"38 Magnets"

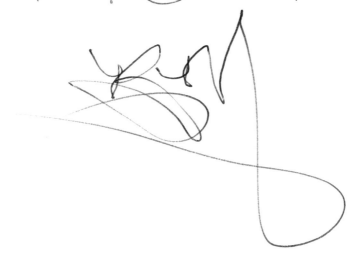

To: Rob

From: Brandon

BRANDON T. MITCHELL

708-518-9945

BRANDON T. MITCHELL

TABLE OF CONTENTS

"38 Magnets"

INTRO-MATION

This is a Publication with 38 thought grabbing stories that speaks volumes, and are backed up by the weapons of scripture, which is the word of God. These magnetic attractions will draw you closer for more. When you complete the readings of this Pioneering Publication, the Author's intentions are for the scholars to become more empowered with wisdom, and to see the ways of life from other perspectives.

I came up with the title, "38 Magnets", to draw a crowd, that are down to Earth, closer to the wisdom that God has given me to share with others. When I was a child, the Lord blessed me with the talent to draw pictures, as an artist. Now, that my years of life have gained wisdom, the Lord has drawn me to the art of writing Power Statements, and craft them into a manuscript, to draw people closer to Him. As "38 Magnets" sounds and looks so much like "38 Magnum", I was drawn to this title for these bulletproof and bullet point reasons:

❖ The irony of this title will draw a person's attraction.

❖ As an iron can be very hot, these are also hot topics to relate to in our everyday life.

❖ These thoughts hit right on bull's-eye, as they are right on target.

❖ I came up with "38 Magnets" to give a limitation to how many stories I will speak on, because the stories that the Lord had blessed me with, has no limits.

❖ As this world is about the use of weapons, I believe this title will gravitate towards more readers.

❖ The spiritual meaning of the number 38 stands for work, or labor. Therefore, this number pertains to the idea of one's calling, and purpose that God has for his or her life (http://www.newhorizonscomchurch.net/upload s/2/3/1/9/23197588/meaning_of_numbers.pdf), which further compliments the justification for me writing this Masterpiece. Each story will grab you like a magnet. There is, also, a spin to each scenario, as "38 Revolvers," that will have you to view attributes from other perspectives.

❖ This is a book with 38 MAGNificEnT stories that will not give you an overkill. Instead, they will give you wisdom and laughter, perhaps, for an extended life.

> *Blessed are ye that hunger now: for ye shall be filled. Blessed are ye that weep now: for ye shall laugh (**Luke 6:21**). Then was our mouth filled with laughter, and our tongue with singing: then said they among the heathen, The LORD hath done great things for them. The LORD hath done great things for us; whereof we are glad (**Psalms 126:2-3**).*

ACKNOWLEDGEMENT

This book is dedicated to my God. It is He who has given me the inspiration to write this book. It allows individuals who read this book to speak, think, laugh, and live a more positive life style.

"38 Magnets"

CHAPTER 1

"FOOD FOR THOUGHT"

"God's Amazing Works"

If you were able to erase your mistakes, to the point were others could not be led/lead to trace your history, how far would you get in life, before your eraser is waivered along with your mistakes? Will you be led/lead to new mistakes with no eraser left, or will you have no drawing back from them?

For you to give a person your direct attention, how would they direct you? If you were instructed by the view of someone's point, you may be drawn to the wrong location. Perhaps, a pencil would have led/lead you in the wrong direction, from someone else's point,

...or maybe you were penciled in on the wrong point of focus, where you were misled.

> *Brethren, I count not myself to have apprehended: but this one thing I do, forgetting those things which are behind, and reaching forth unto those things which are before, I press toward the mark for the prize of the high calling of God in Christ Jesus* **(Philippians 3:13-14)**.

But, God's mission for us is to draw people closer to Him, where He Arts in Heaven.

We can have more class through our Lord. That God is perfect, then why not learn of His perfect will/wheel for our lives. The Lord can pinpoint/pen-point us in the right direction, as He makes no mistakes. A pencil lead can erase; a pen does not erase; and God's word will not erase. Moreover, a pen makes the first and final mark, and so does God. Therefore, His word is final, and it is truth from beginning to end. Furthermore, the blood of Jesus is also the word of truth, and the word of His blood is also final. Therefore, it is stained and red/read for life.

We will see a more beautiful picture of our lives, with the perfect color wheel/will of God, because He gives us light through the Son/sun. The Son/sun comes a cross/across, in our path everyday, to keep us out of darkness. Furthermore, the stars will shed light on our vision to see this world clearly, when we are in darkness. But, the Son/sun freely transfers the possession of light on this world to bring us out of darkness. If it was not for the Son/sun, that's well rounded, to bring us into the light, we would have been drawn to darkness, and led/lead to no Earthly good.

*She obeyed not the voice; she received not correction; she trusted not in the Lord; she drew not near to her God **(Zephaniah 3:2)**. As for God, his way is perfect: the word of the LORD is tried: he is a buckler to all those that trust in him. For who is God save the LORD? Or who is a rock save our God? It is God that girdeth me with strength, and maketh my way perfect. He maketh my feet like hinds' feet, and setteth me upon my high places. He teacheth my hands to war, so that a bow of steel is broken by mine arms. Thou hast also given me the shield of thy salvation: and thy right hand hath holden me up, and thy gentleness hath made me great. Thou hast enlarged my steps under me, that my feet did not slip **(Psalms 18:30-36)**. For the law made nothing perfect, but the bringing in of a better hope did; by the which we draw nigh unto God **(Hebrews 7:19).***

If we stay focused on the Lord, be still, and let God brush upon us, by His perfect will/wheel,

our lives will be painted as a better model, and perhaps, with no strokes, but point by point. But, with God's amazing works, in ways that we mess up in life, He still has a way to keep us in His perfect picture, with life of color, for more than a price.

"SEE THE POINT HOW GOD WILL BRUSH UP ON US?"

(For the redemption of their soul is precious, and it ceaseth for ever:) **(Psalm 49:8)** *Fear ye not therefore, ye are of more value than many sparrows* **(Matthew 10:31)**. *I will make a man more precious than fine gold; even a man than the golden wedge of O'-phir* **(Isaiah 13:12)**. *For what is a man profited, if he shall gain the whole world, and lose his own soul? or what shall a man give in exchange for his soul* **(Matthew 16:26)**?

"What Shoes Are You Wearing"

When you go to a shoe store, and try on a new pair of shoes, are they really new, or do they have a spell on them, from someone else's walk? It has been said, "You aren't in my shoes!" In other words, "Don't judge me by my steps if you have not walked my path of life."

> *WHOSE MOUTH IS FULL OF CURSING AND BITTERNESS: THEIR FEET ARE SWIFT TO SHED BLOOD: DESTRUCCTION AND MISERY ARE IN THEIR WAYS: AND THE WAY OF PEACE HAVE THEY NOT KNOWN* **(Romans 3:14-17)**: *Judge not, that ye be not judged* **(Matthew 7:1)**. *Who art thou that judgest another man's servant? to his own master he standeth or falleth. Yea, he shall be holden up: for God is able to make him stand* **(Romans 14:4)**.

How many feet have been in the shoes that you are trying on?

Are you under a spell to walk in their path, or do you wash your feet to be cleansed of another person's ways? Perhaps, you wish to continue in their germ-ney (journey) and follow the foot steps of another person's paths, by being in their walks. Before you try on a pair of shoes, do you know the paths that they have already taken? Furthermore, do you know the paths that others have taken in these same shoes, before you decide to try and pair up with them? If there are foot stains in those shoes, before you have tried them on, then whose toes are you stepping on? Can their kicks knock you out?

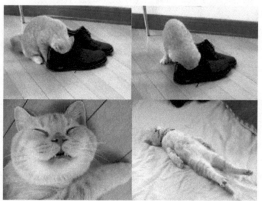

**The walks of this world stinks.
There's no wonder why we put the blame
on the shoes, when our shoes are feet
away from the nose.**

Wherein in time past ye walked according to the course of this world, according to the prince of the power of the air, the spirit that now worketh in the children of disobedience: Among whom also we all had our conversation in times past in the lusts of our flesh, fulfilling the desires of the flesh and of the mind; and were by nature the children of wrath, even as others **(Ephesians 2:2-3)**.

When you put gym shoes in the washer, don't they start to shrink? Perhaps, is it that troubles from the walks of those shoes being washed away? Even if so, the stains are still there.

Have you ever gotten smoked in a race while having on a pair of running shoes, or track shoes? Were the shoes smelly after the race, and did you get a little high from the smoke, and not see where you were going? Why would you run errands that God has not called you to relay? Is that why there are delays? Don't marinade in someone else's season that is too hot or spicy for you to handle. Why judge another person's walk, and the soles of their shoes are too slippery for your walk? But, it's funny how we use the term, "Those are some smooth shoes." But, we can't handle a slide on film, where you slipped up, trying to handle the smooth walks of another person's journey?

"IF YOU CAN SLIP ON SOME NICE SHOES, WOULD THAT ALTER YOUR WALK?"

Perhaps, you would feel foolish, in knowing the price you would have paid, by running around in someone else's slippery shoes, and they have you on a slide, to show a rerun. Perhaps, the slick shoes captured your attention. But, if we can put taps on our own shoes, we won't have to worry about stumbling over our own feet. Moreover, God wants us to tap into His word, where He will be our guide, for a better walk with Him.

> *For thou hast delivered my soul from death: wilt not thou deliver my feet from falling, that I may walk before God in the light of the living* **(Psalm 56:13)**?

We also speak the term, "Those are some hot shoes!"

But, why wear them if they are so hot? Aren't they too hot for your feet to handle? Also, do you know the heat that one has walked through, being in those shoes that may be a hot price to pay? Why would you walk into someone else's fire?

> *Behold, all ye that kindle a fire, that compass yourselves about with sparks: walk in the light of your fire, and in the sparks that ye have kindled. This shall ye have of mine hand; ye shall lie down in sorrow* **(Isaiah 50:11)**.

Moreover, from the day that you had started your journey, in your first pair of shoes ever worn, until now; have anyone followed your exact foot steps of life, besides your shadow? Furthermore, that we all may have some crazy ways, that's not of God, and if your shadow had a mind of its own, would it follow you to loose its own life, if you decided to loose yours by jumping off of a cliff? If you want someone else to shadow your footsteps, you have to first of all respect yourself, and your own shadow.

When you follow the foot steps of God, He will give you a brand-new pair of shoes that are only meant for you to wear. As we are all put on Earth for our own unique purpose, the shoes that are for you, no one can steal your walks in which you are ordained for. The soles of your shoes are supposed to be the example of your walk, to reach souls for God.

*O L<small>ORD</small>, I know that the way of man is not in himself: it is not in man that walketh to direct his steps **(Jeremiah 10:23)**. The steps of a good man are ordered by the L<small>ORD</small>: and he delighteth in his way. Though he fall, he shall not be utterly cast down: for the L<small>ORD</small> upholdeth him with his hand **(Psalms 37:23-24)**. For we are his workmanship, created in Christ Jesus unto good works, which God hath before ordained that we should walk in them **(Ephesians 2:10)**.*

It's funny when people speak the slang term, "Those are some tight shoes!"

But, why wear them if they are so tight? When your shoes are too tight on your feet, do your feet feel broken, or do you break in your shoes before they break into you? Furthermore, if you don't break your shoes in before you wear them out, then before you go on break, they will wear you out. Why wear a pair of shoes that will steal your joy? Why give shoes authority over your walk, when God has given you dominion over all things? A pair of shoes is supposed to be under your submission.

If you are under the submission of shoes, will they not be over your head?

If shoes were over your head,
they would walk all over you.

Perhaps, that's why our issues (is-shoes) that we encounter are based on our walk. But, God has given us dominion over all shoes, for them to submit to us. When we have issues of life, that are hard to walk in, then we should go to God, and not have tight strings attached.

That's why, we give God more room to complete our walk. With the Lord, we have the authority to take our shoes through every step of our lives, so they will not miss a beat, as we walk from the soul/sole and from the heart.

> *Take my yoke upon you, and learn of me; for I am meek and lowly in heart: and ye shall find rest unto your souls (**Matthew 11:29**).*

Are the soles of your shoes, that you stand firm to, heeled strong enough for your spiritual walk, or for your walk in them?

IF YOU INTEND TO MAKE YOURSELF TALL TO BRING OTHERS DOWN, GOD WILL BREAK YOU DOWN.

If your shoes aren't strong enough to keep you lifted up, then you will be downsized to a lower level. There are times that you will have to take your shoes off in order to solely depend on the Lord through praise, to lift you higher.

> *So the spirit lifted me up, and took me away, and I went in bitterness, in the heat of my spirit; but the hand of the LORD was strong upon me (**Ezekiel 3:14**). And the spirit entered into me when he spake unto me,*

and set me upon my feet, that I heard him that spake unto me (Ezekiel 2:2). The Lord upholdeth all that fall, and raiseth up all those that be bowed down (Psalm 145:14).

Is your soul healed to continue the walk, in which God has ordained for you, or do you have strongholds? On the other hand, when you are too uptight to give God your time, are you not disconnected from Him? On that note, if God made time, then who do you depend on to be your watch? Moreover, if God works over time/overtime, then He watches over you.

And God said, Let there be lights in the firmament of the heaven to divide the day from the night; and let them be for signs, and for seasons, and for days, and years: And let them be for lights in the firmament of the heaven to give light upon the earth: and it was so. And God made two great lights; the greater light to rule the day, and the lesser light to rule the night: he *made the stars also. And God set them in the firmament of the heaven to give light upon the earth, And to rule over the day and over the night, and to divide the light from the darkness: and God saw that it was good **(Genesis 1:14-18)**. I will instruct thee and teach thee in the way which thou shalt go: I will guide thee with mine eye **(Psalm 32:8)**.*

When your shoes are tied up too tightly, isn't there discomfort in your walk, more and more, as time permits? But, if you are tied up too much, to walk with God, isn't there discomfort in your path to walk the straight narrow road of life? Maybe you're tied up, with your back against the wall.

Perhaps, you are being smoked by defeat, and can't see your journey ahead. Are you looking for an accident to happen, to be towed/toed/told away? Why not be directed by God, who have told/toed us a way, time and time again, by directing our walk?

> Thy word is a lamp unto my feet, and a light unto my path **(Psalm 119:105)**.

The shoes that you are trying on, or so desperate to wear, are they really brand spanking new, or do you get a spanking by wearing the brand named shoes, that has a spell on them, which is not in your name, to walk you down a wrong path? Were the shoes that you tried on, walked by someone else in a short distance, from the rack, down the aisle, and back? Perhaps, they were marinated in someone else's walk for a longer distance in time, before they were brought back to the rack. Were they still price tagged the same?

As we were born with a different number (Social Security number) from birth, we have all worn shoes that's had a price tag on them. Whose life are you walking in? Moreover, whose name are you walking in? The sun made by God is the highest and hottest that we, as a nation, have seen. But, the Son of God has been through the hottest times, and paid the highest price for our sins. Who wants to pay the price of Jesus' name, by being in His walks of life?

> Therefore we are buried with him by baptism into death: that like as Christ was raised up from the dead by the glory of the Father, even so we also should walk in newness of life **(Romans 6:4)**.

"The Left Piece, Centerpiece, Or The Right Piece"

If all of life is right, then what is left to make us stronger? Shouldn't we have balance on both sides? Now, if we were the center, between left and right, and the left side was cold, and the right side was hot, wouldn't we be lukewarm?

Cold   Lukewarm   Hot

So then because thou art lukewarm, and neither cold nor hot, I will spue thee out of my mouth ***(Revelation 3:16)***.

Moreover, if all of our rights were left behind, and we could not turn back, then wouldn't we soon come to a dead end, with no where else to turn, or no one else to turn to?

IF DOORS BEHIND YOU ARE SHUT, AND ONLY A DEAD END IS IN FRONT OF YOU, THEN HOW CAN YOU TURN BACK TO REROUTE YOUR LIFE?

If everything that was right was left behind you, then what challenges are before you, to make you stronger? Now, if everything that you had left was right behind you, then wouldn't you feel stalked? Perhaps, you will be the centerpiece of man's focus to destroy you. But, we are also the centerpiece of God's focus, to make us better, for His glory.

People have been judged for walking on two left feet, by conveying that they cannot dance.

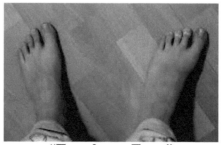

"TWO LEFT FEET"

But, does it make them better, if both of there feet were right?

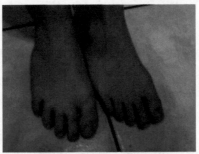

"Two Right Feet"

Does that necessarily make their spiritual walk correct? If you had two left feet, then perhaps, that may cause you to be left behind the others. But, if you had two right feet, then maybe that would make you right behind the others? Now, if both of your feet are correct, one left and one right, doesn't mean that your spiritual walk is correct through God? Just maybe, your right foot would have to tell the left foot what to do, especially if the right foot speaks volumes. Moreover, if your feet were corrected through a doctor, from surgery, by his specifications, does not mean that they're in right standings. God did not design our walk to come to a dead end. Our Father made us to be in His perfect image, but He did not make us to be perfect. Instead, God designed hope through our mistakes and shortcomings.

> *I THEREFORE, the prisoner of the Lord, beseech you that ye walk worthy of the vocation wherewith ye are called* **(Ephesians 4:1)**. *And he said unto me, My grace is sufficient for thee: for my strength is made perfect in weakness. Most gladly therefore will I rather glory in my infirmities, that the power of Christ may rest upon me* **(2 Corinthians 12:9)**.

How many people have played the game of chess? Isn't it something how people put their hearts into the game of chess more seriously than life itself?

It is made their center focus. But, God gave us a life, as we all have a chest with a heart in the center. We are all His focus and His centerpiece where we stand. With that being said, shouldn't we all make God our center focus, from our hearts for peace and eternal life through Him? God plays no games with us, but He gives us game for life, to stay strong, and to continue our walk with Him.

> *Trust in the LORD with all thine heart; and lean not unto thine own understanding. In all thy ways acknowledge him, and he shall direct thy paths* **(Proverbs 3:5-6)**. *The spirit of God hath made me, and the breath of the Almighty hath given me life* **(Job 33:4)**. *And this is the record, that God hath given to us eternal life, and this life is in his Son* **(1 John 5:11)**.

"Seeing Past The Seashore"

A vision will come through a see/sea. That water has a refection, perhaps it was created for a see/sea of beauty.

But, if you can get over the sees/seas of this world, then you can move by faith, and not by sight. Isn't most of this world surrounded by the waters? If you go by a see/sea, a see/sea will only go so far. But, if you go by faith, you will go farther than a see/sea. If you put your faith in God, for His will in your life, He will take you farther than you can see/sea. God will take you over-sees/overseas.

> *Then thou shalt see, and flow together, and thine heart shall fear, and be enlarged; because the abundance of the sea shall be converted unto thee, the forces of the Gentiles shall come unto thee **(Isaiah 60:5)**.*

Therefore, by God's will, you can overcome your mind, to not be drowned in your own thoughts. If you can't come up higher in the Lord, then do you have the faith to walk across the waters on your own, or does your eyes take away your faith, to walk over a see/sea?

> *So when they had rowed about five and twenty or thirty furlongs, they see Jesus walking on the sea, and drawing nigh unto the ship: and they were afraid* ***(John 6:19)****.*

If you walk by sight, and not by faith, then whose site will you walk on? Furthermore, whose side will you walk on, or which walk will you decide on?

ENTER YE IN AT THE STRAIT GATE: FOR WIDE IS THE GATE, AND BROAD IS THE WAY, THAT LEADETH TO DESTRUCTION, AND MANY THERE BE WHICH GO IN THEREAT (MATTHEW 7:13).

BECAUSE STRAIT IS THE GATE, AND NARROW IS THE WAY, WHICH LEADETH UNTO LIFE, AND FEW THERE BE THAT FIND IT (MATTHEW 7:14).

> *(For we walk by faith, not by sight:) We are confident, I say, and willing rather to be absent from the body, and to be present with the Lord. Wherefore we labour, that, whether present or absent, we may be accepted of him* ***(2 Corinthians 5:7-9)****.*

Will you be in a danger zone where there is destruction of a tearing down of a building, or are you walking by faith, to a building up of positive strongholds, that can't be knocked down? In this scenario, positive strongholds are referred to as holding strong onto the Lord. But, if negative strongholds can add up, to make you stronger, then what is weighing you down?

> *Now faith is the substance of things hoped for, the evidence of things not seen **(Hebrews 11:1)**. While we look not at the things which are seen, but at the things which are not seen: for the things which are seen are temporal; but the things which are not seen are eternal **(2 Corinthians 4:18)**.*

To elaborate, if negative strongholds may add up, to be positive, then aren't we suppose to count the negatives in our lives as all joy?

> *My brethren, count it all joy when ye fall into divers temptations; Knowing this, that the trying of your faith worketh patience **(James 1:2-3)**. Therefore I take pleasure in infirmities, in reproaches, in necessities, in persecutions, in distresses for Christ's sake: for when I am weak, then am I strong **(2 Corinthians 12:10)**.*

Moreover, when you walk by faith, and not by sight, you will have to recite what you want, by the power of your tongue. If you don't recite what you want by faith, you will continue to recite/reside where you are, and prolong your case.

> *And Jesus answering saith unto them, Have faith in God. For verily I say unto you, That whosoever shall say unto this mountain, Be thou removed, and be thou cast into the sea; and shall not doubt in his heart, but shall believe that those things which he saith shall come to pass; he shall have whatsoever he saith. Therefore I say unto you, What things soever ye desire, when ye pray, believe that ye receive them, and ye shall have them **(Mark 11:22-24)**.*

If you say, "I am going to go with God", then you are also saying, "I will go with God". Therefore, if God is "I Am", then shouldn't He be your will? You can overcome every obstacle in life, for every situation, as far, and as long as you can see/sea your way through Christ. If you have the ability to walk across the waters of a see/sea, without fear, as Peter once tried, and not be distracted by the winds, then you can go all the way with Christ the first time instead of making this a repeater's/re-Peter's course. Isn't the far distance that you go with God also the long distance with God? For every circumstance that you will come to see/sea your way through, by the guidance of God, you can pass to walk assured/a shore.

> *And in the fourth watch of the night Jesus went unto them, walking on the sea. And when the disciples saw him walking on the sea, they were troubled, saying, It is a spirit; and they cried out for fear. But straightway Jesus spake unto them, saying, Be of good cheer; it is I; be not afraid. And Peter answered him and said, Lord, if it be thou, bid me come unto thee on the water. And he said, Come. And when Peter was come down out of the ship, he walked on the water, to go to Jesus. But when he saw the wind boisterous, he was afraid; and beginning to sink, he cried, saying, Lord, save me. And immediately Jesus stretched forth his hand, and caught him, and said unto him, O thou of little faith, wherefore didst thou doubt* **(Matthew 14:25-31)**?

"Celebrating A Broken Record"

It's funny how we celebrate an occasion for someone breaking a record in sports. But, why is it that we feel the need to celebrate over a broken record, versus celebrating over a stronger record that's harder to break? Are the athletes trying to beat their competitors until they break them, before they cross the finish line? That the challenger has a heart to compete, are you trying to break their heart, so that you can tape a recording of it, over and over?

*Know ye not that they which run in a race run all, but one receiveth the prize? So run, that ye may obtain. And every man that striveth for the mastery is temperate in all things. Now they do it to obtain a corruptible crown; but we an incorruptible. I therefore so run, not as uncertainly; so fight I, not as one that beateth the air **(1 Corinthians 9:24-26)**: He shall break in pieces mighty men without number, and set others in their stead **(Job 34:24)**. But now they break down the carved work thereof at once with axes and hammers **(Psalm 74:6)**.*

Why break your brother's record that he worked so hard to pay the price for, instead of helping your brother in this race called life? If you take over the torch, by giving your brother a helping hand, you can both stay on track.

If breaking someone's best record sounds like music to your ears, then how would you like if someone had broken the record to your favorite song?

The Jews therefore, because it was the preparation, that the bodies should not remain upon the cross on the sabbath day, (for that sabbath day was an high day,) besought Pilate that their legs might be broken, and that they might be taken away. Then came the soldiers, and brake the legs of the first, and of the other which was crucified with him. But, when they came to Jesus, and saw that he was dead already, they brake not his legs: But one of the soldiers with a spear pierced his side, and forthwith came there out blood and water. And he that saw it bare record, and his record is true: and he knoweth that he saith true, that ye might believe. For these things were done, that the scripture should be, A BONE OF HIM SHALL NOT BE BROKEN **(John 19:31-36)**.

Looking from another perspective, many people have spoken the term, "I have a bone to pick with you." Does a person feel the need to pick a bone with someone, to get underneath their skin?

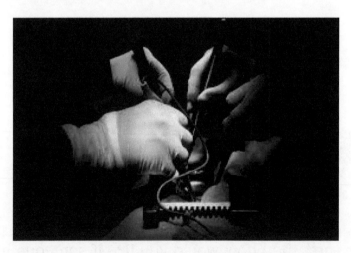

Is someone trying to skele/scale them down to grab the joy out of their heart until it is broken, or is the person trying to skull them down with the skill of mind games?

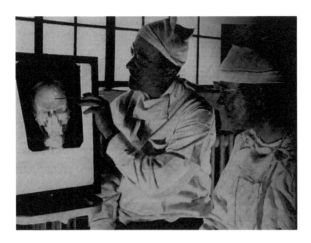

Maybe, he's just being a wise guy.

> *Make me to hear joy and gladness; that the bones which thou hast broken may rejoice. Hide thy face from my sins, and blot out all mine iniquities. Create in me a clean heart, O God; and renew a right spirit within me* **(Psalms 51:8-10)**. *By long forbearing is a prince persuaded, and a soft tongue breaketh the bone* **(Proverbs 25:15)**. *Behold, my servants shall sing for joy of heart, but ye shall cry for sorrow of heart, and shall howl for vexation of spirit* **(Isaiah 65:14)**. *A wise man scaleth the city of the mighty, and casteth down the strength of the confidence thereof* **(Proverbs 21:22)**.

Why is it that a person works so hard to break into someone's heart, or fraud into their mind, instead of helping that person to strengthen their heart, and encourage positive thoughts? Does a person find it a pleasure to reach for someone else's joy? Maybe, they want to see a mind destroyed, and a heart broken, as they do a record. Furthermore, why not plan on breaking Satan's record against us, since his plan is to break us from our livelihood? The adversary is our real enemy.

> *And whatsoever ye do, do it heartily, as to the Lord, and not unto men (**Colossians 3:23**); But rejoice, inasmuch as ye are partakers of Christ's sufferings; that, when his glory shall be revealed, ye may be glad also with exceeding joy (**1 Peter 4:13**). Be sober, be vigilant; because your adversary the devil, as a roaring lion, walketh about, seeking whom he may devour: Whom resist stedfast in the faith, knowing that the same afflictions are accomplished in your brethren that are in the world (**1 Peter 5:8-9**).*

Breaking a person's record, seems to work hand in hand, with the reason that an athlete puts all of their heart and mind into it.

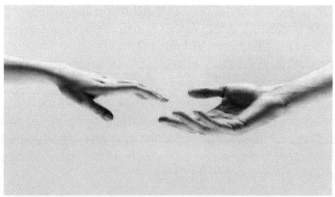

Why separate with a torch when you can run in this life together, hand in hand? If two partners, on the same team, will keep hand in hand, then how can a heart be broken? Moreover, how can their record be broken if both partners are firm together as one whole/hold?

Is the heart and mind in good hands? Moreover, is the athlete putting all of their own heart and mind into it, to reach for a goal/gold,

or do they have a mind to reach for someone else's heart in which they want to own? Maybe you are reaching for a broken record that's placed around a gold.

If someone medal's/meddles with you, and you see yourself as a gold, silver, or bronze, then who's there to steal/steel your joy, if your joy is in your heart? Moreover, if each part of your life is connected to a clip (as a part in a movie), then what is your life hooked on?

IS YOUR LIFE CLIPPED TO BRONZE, SILVER, OR GOLD MEMORIES? HOW DOES YOUR LIFE SHINE? MOREOVER, HOW DOES YOUR LIGHT SHINE ON OTHERS?

   Is your life stabled/stapled as firm as you would like it to be?

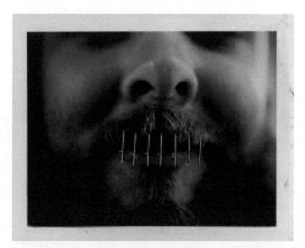

MANY TIMES SILENCE IS THE BEST OPTION TO KEEP YOUR LIFE FIRMLY STABLE/STAPLED.

Furthermore, do you keep a record on file, in your mind, of bad things that have happened, or do you have those file/foul memories broken, for a breakthrough to joy?

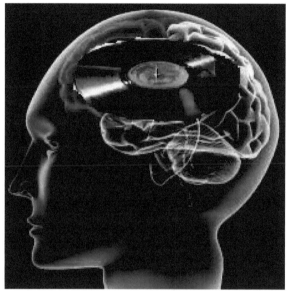

A RECORD THAT SKIPS TO PLAY OVER AND OVER, IN YOUR MIND, WILL CONTINUE AS A BROKEN RECORD. BUT, WITHOUT GOLDEN MEMORIES!

*Let all bitterness, and wrath, and anger, and clamour, and evil speaking, be put away from you, with all malice: And be ye kind one to another, tenderhearted, forgiving one another, even as God for Christ's sake hath forgiven you **(Ephesians 4:31-32)**.*

"Whose Will And Whose Way Are You In?"

It has been said, "Where there's a will, there's a way." But, that comes to the question, "In whose will/wheel are you established, or whose way are you in? Are you in another person's way, or are you in the ways of God? If God is not your will/wheel, then who is driving you crazy? Are you behind a will/wheel that may lead you down the wrong path, or is the path that you are being driven, going uphill or downhill? If it is hard to say, without a clue, then perhaps, there are no signs for your wonders. But, if you let God's will/wheel be your guide, you will never be lost. He will take you through to an eternal path, with many signs and wonders that will never lead you astray.

*God also bearing them witness, both with signs and wonders, and with divers miracles, and gifts of the Holy Ghost, according to his own will **(Hebrews 2:4)**? As for God, his way is perfect; the word of the Lord is tried: he is a buckler to all them that trust in him **(2 Samuel 22:31)**. Deliver me not over unto the will of mine enemies: for false witnesses are risen up against me, and such as breathe out cruelty **(Psalm 27:12)**.*

Have you done the math to find out if a will/wheel is giving you drive on a positive axis, or negative axis? In which direction do you have access? Moreover, do you have a strong family tree? There can be a situation where you tend to be bound from going any place, where you may feel stuck at zero (0).

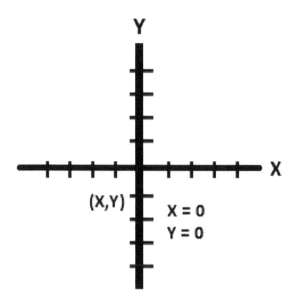

You aren't moving up or down, nor back or forth. Perhaps, it depends on your actions of life that chooses your destiny. If your "Act" is what you do in life, and an "Ion (Biophysical term) is the body's electrical energy source for gain or loss, then what are your Act-Ions (actions)? Moreover, what are your "I-Act-Ons"? Furthermore, what is your Bio (Biography)? If your performance determines your destiny in life, then what is your ACT score? But, does an ACT test determine your destiny over God's act in your life?

There are times that people get to a certain point in life, but can't seem to move further, whether it's forward or moving up. They may feel at a stand still. What point are you?

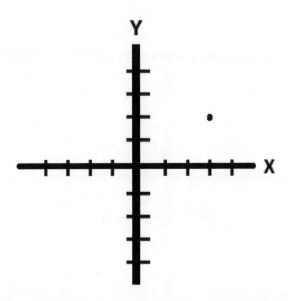

Why stay at the same level in life, when you can have a higher access/axis to "Y"? At times, we may have to take X-amount of steps to move forward in life, but going to a higher plane (surface), on the Y-axis, you will have to go through a test of acts, to move by faith, and not ask Y/why. But, if you continue life, only on the X-axis, you will remain on a plain/plane surface that will never change.

> *By whom also we have access by faith into this grace wherein we stand, and rejoice in hope of the glory of God (**Romans 5:2**).*

That no man has the since/cents to write the Bible, he doesn't have the change to write the Bible. Furthermore, if no man can right the Bible, then no one can afford to tell it wrong. Moreover, how can we write/right the Bible, if we have no since of direction without God? It makes since/cents to keep quiet. To stay quiet is wisdom, and wisdom is rich, because it has worth. Therefore, the more wisdom that one builds in silence is a gain for more change, as a deposit to trust with. Perhaps, that's why wisdom is trustworthy.

*That their hearts might be comforted, being knit together in love, and unto all riches of the full assurance of understanding, to the acknowledgement of the mystery of God, and of the Father, and of Christ; In whom are hid all the treasures of wisdom and knowledge **(Colossians 2:2-3)**. The fear of the LORD is the beginning of knowledge: but fools despise wisdom and instruction **(Proverbs 1:7)**. Wisdom is the principal thing; therefore get wisdom: and with all thy getting get understanding **(Proverbs 4:7)**. Happy is the man that findeth wisdom, and the man that getteth understanding. For the merchandise of it is better than the merchandise of silver, and the gain thereof than fine gold **(Proverbs 3:13-14)**. A fool uttereth all his mind: but a wise man keepeth it in till afterwards **(Proverbs 29:11)**. He that keepeth his mouth keepeth his life: but he that openeth wide his lips shall have destruction **(Proverbs 13:3)**. He that trusteth in his own heart is a fool: but whoso walketh wisely, he shall be delivered **(Proverbs 28:26)**.*

If you come into an agreement with a circle of people, whose circle are you in? Are you in a circle with positive people, that are believers of Christ, or are you in a negative circle, with unbelievers against Christ, that have pulled you into their setups, that will eventually turn to upsets?

Positive side of battery
(+)
Negative side of battery
(-)

If you are in a positive circle, then your circle-stance/circumstance will be charged with positive energy.
If you are in a negative circle, then the charge against you may be a battery with assault.

> *I the LORD search the heart, I try the reins, even to give every man according to his ways, and according to the fruit of his doings* **(Jeremiah 17:10)**.

On the contrary, even though a battery has two different worlds (a positive and a negative), they agree to disagree, and continue to operate with life through other substances. But, when we, as individuals, come to a disagreement, we seem to disagree to agree, to the degree where we are charged with a battery. Isn't it amazing how much a battery can teach us, besides being charged, or besides being dead? That we have life and charge over any battery, when we are charged with a battery, perhaps, that's an insult/assault.

If you are in agreement with an individual, then what is the circumstance? Have you taken a look at the circle, as well as the agreement? What part of the pie/Π do you receive, or where is the mediator?

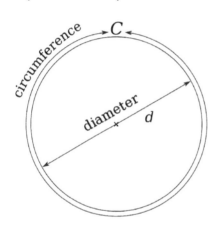

$$Π = C/d$$

Mediator and diameter are closely related.

Mediator vs Diameter

mediator ≈ diameter
me(dia)tor ≈ diameter
dia-me-tor ≈ diameter

Mediator *is a person who mediates between Parties; A person who divides down the middle.* **Diameter** *is a straight line passing through the center of a circle or sphere and meeting the circumference or surface at each end.*

For there is one God, and one mediator between God and men, the man Christ Jesus **(1 Timothy 2:5)***;*

If we can become a team with an agreement in prayer, we can have power. It is good to move forward on the *X-axis*, but God also wants us to rise to new heights, on the *Y-axis*.

$$X^y = \text{"X" to the "y" power.}$$

How far are you willing to move forward in life, and to what power are you planning to rise? When two or more come together in agreement, there is power. But, if *"X"* is by itself, or *"Y"* is lonely, then there is no one to power with. An *"X"* will just be an *"X"*, and a *"Y"* will just be a *"Y"*.

The higher the power, the stronger the test. With that being said, if we have not past all of the test that we have been given, here on Earth, then how is it that we feel so ready to be with God, where it takes a higher power of test to go through than the one's that we have yet to pass?

> *Blessed is the man that endureth temptation: for when he is tried, he shall receive the crown of life, which the Lord hath promised to them that love him* ***(James 1:12)***. *That the trial of your faith, being much more precious than of gold that perisheth, though it be tried with fire, might be found unto praise and honour and glory at the appearing of Jesus Christ* ***(1 Peter 1:7)***: *For we are labourers together with God: ye are God's husbandry, ye are God's building. According to the grace of God which is given unto me, as a wise masterbuilder, I have laid the foundation, and another buildeth thereon. But let every man take heed how he buildeth thereupon. For other foundation can no man lay than that is laid, which is Jesus Christ* ***(1 Corinthians 3:9-11)***.

If we operate by faith, then we can accomplish all things through Christ who strengthens us. But, if God did not design faith, then on a "*X*" and "*Y*" axis, will a building stand the test? Furthermore, if the "*X-axis*" and "*Y-axis*" was not formed as a cross (of life), would we be able to stand the falls of life, without balance?

> *Verily I say unto you, Whatsoever ye shall bind on earth shall be bound in heaven: and whatsoever ye shall loose on earth shall be loosed in heaven. Again I say unto you, That if two of you shall agree on earth as touching any thing that they shall ask, it shall be done for them of my Father which is in heaven. For where two or three are gathered together in my name, there am I in the midst of them* **(Matthew 18:18-20)**.

"My Cell Phone Went Dead"

It's funny how people will say, "My cell phone went dead." Why is it that a person speaks death into a device that becomes useful at any given moment?

*Death and life are in the power of the tongue: and they that love it shall eat the fruit thereof (**Proverbs 18:21**).*

A cell phone works by juice, and juice is power. If a cell phone has no power, then it cannot function for another word to be spoken. It would have to be plugged in. But, doesn't a word have power?

If we are not plugged into God's word, then how much power are we losing? Furthermore, as we speak with the members of our mouths, into a cell phone, isn't a cell phone losing its life, unless it is plugged in? Moreover, if God created us with cells to function, then why not call on Him to be charged?

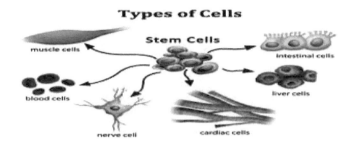

Even so the tongue is a little member, and boasteth great things. Behold, how great a matter a little fire kindleth! And the tongue is a fire, a world of iniquity: so is the tongue among our members, that it defileth the whole body, and setteth on fire the course of nature; and it is set on fire of hell **(James 3:5-6)**. *He that keepeth his mouth keepeth his life: but he that openeth wide his lips shall have destruction* **(Proverbs 13:3)**. *Ever learning, and never able to come to the knowledge of the truth* **(2 Timothy 3:7)**.

If we have a better, stronger, and a more prosperous life than a cell phone, then how come a cell phone's reception has more word than each one of us? Does that sound like a sellout/cell out? A cell phone is more receptive to man's word, that is not always true, than man is accepting to God's word, that is truth in all ways. A cell phone will quote what a man or woman would send through a text, more so than a person would quote God's word through trials and a test. In other words, a cell phone usually has no problem delivering a message by a man or a woman, but there are many times that the masters of cell phones will not submit to delivering God's word, who is our Master.

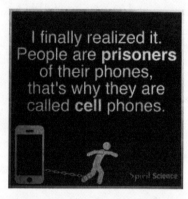

A man told me one day in a text message, "Please, forgive me for any misspelled words or incorrect grammar." This was sent to my cell phone. I replied in conversed words, "I won't hold you accountable for misspelled grammar. Neither will I hold your cell phone accountable for errors. If I held either one of our cell phones accountable for every mistake, then I may not have a call on my life.

> *"Be not thou therefore ashamed of the testimony of our Lord, nor of me his prisoner: but be thou partaker of the afflictions of the gospel according to the power of God; Who hath saved us, and called us with an holy calling, not according to our works, but according to his own purpose and grace, which was given us in Christ Jesus before the world began* **(2 Timothy 1:8-9)**, *For the gifts and calling of God are without repentance* **(Romans 11:29)**.

When two men are debating against each other, whether it's a friendly debate, or debating on harsh terms, they may speak with slang terminology. Mic may say to Will, "I don't think you have the juice to speak against me." Will would respond, "Where there's a will, there's a way." If juice is to power, then who has the most word to conquer victory, Will or Mic?

WILL   **MIC**

Will can turn a mic off, but Mic doesn't have the power to stop a will. A mic cannot speak by itself. Therefore, without a word, it has no power. Someone will have to speak up in its place/base. But, a will has the power of attorney, and it can speak for itself. We should have that same attitude for God's word. His word is our will. It is, also, our juice (as the fruit of the spirit), which is the power source for our energy, so that we will not go dead.

A will = Juice = Power

But, it never fells, many people wants to be like Mic. But, will it ever stand? On that note, God's will stands forever.

> *Now unto him that is able to do exceeding abundantly above all that we ask or think, according to the power that worketh in us **(Ephesians 3:20)**, And he said unto me, My grace is sufficient for thee: for my strength is made perfect in weakness. Most gladly*

therefore will I rather glory in my infirmities, that the power of Christ may rest upon me (2 Corinthians 12:9).

If a cell phone is dead, it will be no longer useful. Speaking of a cell phone being so useful, to the point that we can't live without it, aren't the cells that we were created with more important? Keeping them functioning will maintain our lives. God has given each one of us the ability to charge and empower ourselves, through His word.

If we are prisoners of our cell phones, and the word of God is in each cell, then why not get lock into God's word for protection over our lives, and look for His call? Moreover, we have the ability to charge and empower our lives through the cells of Jesus' blood.

According as his divine power hath given unto us all things that pertain unto life and godliness, through the knowledge of him that hath called us to glory and virtue (2 Peter 1:3): For the life of the flesh is in the blood: and I have given it to you upon the altar to make an atonement for your souls: for it is the blood that maketh an atonement for the soul (Leviticus 17:11).

45

A cell phone connection to the internet is fed from Wi-Fi. But, isn't Wi-Fi and a cell phone created by man? Once again, aren't our blood cells created by God? If we were created by the same Father in Heaven, then why do we treat our cell phones with more value than our brothers and sisters in Christ?

A cell phone dressed in a tuxedo!

Who hath saved us, and called us with an holy calling, not according to our works, but according to his own purpose and grace, which was given us in Christ Jesus before the world began, But is now made manifest by the appearing of our Saviour Jesus Christ, who hath abolished death, and hath brought life and immortality to light through the gospel **(2 Timothy 1:9-10)**:

When a person has a chip on their shoulder, don't they start acting up? When a cell phone has a built in chip, doesn't it get activated? When we have a chip on our shoulder, are we doing everything that we are supposed to do through our Lord? On the other hand, when a FM radio chip is installed into a cell phone, to whom is a cell phone controlled by?

A. It's Master (you)
B. The Chip
C. Both

*No man can serve two masters: for either he will hate the one, and love the other; or else he will hold to the one, and despise the other. Ye can not serve God and mammon **(Matthew 6:24)**. Take heed, brethren, lest there be in any of you an evil heart of unbelief, in departing from the living God. But exhort one another daily, while it is called To day; lest any of you be hardened through the deceitfulness of sin **(Hebrews 3:12-13)**.*

It's something how a cell phone device can randomly call any number it wants to call, while it is in your pocket, without your permission. Is it dialing numbers on its own, or does your pocket tell your cell phone who to call on? If your pocket has the keys to success, then perhaps, your cell phone is controlled by the keys of your pocket. I would be sure to keep it away from my wallet. If we have a better life than a cell phone device, then how come we are not controlled by the keys of God's word, which is the entrance to His kingdom? A cell phone device will make many false calls that we may bet our lives on. But, with God, He has a true calling on each of our lives that we can live on. Why do we doubt Him?

*When he shall come to be glorified in his saints, and to be admired in all them that believe (because our testimony among you was believed) in that day. Wherefore also we pray always for you, that our God would count you worthy of this calling, and fulfil all the good pleasure of his goodness, and the work of faith with power: That the name of our Lord Jesus Christ may be glorified in you, and ye in him, according to the grace of our God and the Lord Jesus Christ **(2 Thessalonians 1:10-12)**. There is one body, and one Spirit, even as ye are called in one hope of your calling; One Lord, one faith, one baptism, One God and*

Father of all, who is above all, and through all, and in you all (Ephesians 4:4-6), There are many devices in a man's heart; nevertheless the counsel of the LORD, that shall stand (Proverbs 19:21). That your faith should not stand in the wisdom of men, but in the power of God (1 Corinthians 2:5). Jesus answered, Verily, verily, I say unto thee, Except a man be born of water and of the Spirit, he cannot enter into the kingdom of God (John 3:5).

It's funny that a person would say, "I feel naked without my cell phone." How can a small device give any person that much coverage? Will we feel left out in the cold if we left our cell phones at home? Does Satan have the cell of your mind on every page, and every thought that is paged to you on your cell phone? Perhaps, we will miss out on a hot message that would have gotten us heated, or fired up.

"A SMOKING HOT MESSAGE"

Therefore, we would go home to get our cell phone devices to feel covered in a hot mess (hot message). But, why is it that when we forget our bibles, we keep going when we know that God has a call for each one of us, that's not through a cell/sell/sale? But, if we are sold out for God, then our lives will sail smooth.

> There is one body, and one Spirit, even as ye are called in one hope of your calling **(Ephesians 4:4)**;

Will not He keep us covered and protected? A cell phone can fit into our hand and pocket. But, we can fit into the grace of God's right hand, and be left covered in His other hand.

> Thou art my hiding place and my shield: I hope in thy word **(Psalm 119:114)**. Even there shall thy hand lead me, and thy right hand shall hold me **(Psalm 139:10)**.

Moreover, a cell phone will run out of power, and will need to be charged, but God is always on charge for us. Even when we're asleep, He never runs out of power.

> And what is the exceeding greatness of his power to us-ward who believe, according to the working of his mighty power, Which he wrought in Christ, when he raised him from the dead, and set him at his own right hand in the heavenly places, Far above all principality, and power, and might, and dominion, and every name that is named, not only in this world, but also in that which is to come **(Ephesians 1:19-21)**:

On the other hand, there are more people using there cell phones to key in the scripture readings, during church service or bible study. If a cell phone is dropped into water, then it will be dead, because the cell phone will no longer be useful. But, when we are dropped into the water, through Jesus Christ, we are born again.

*And now why tarriest thou? arise, and be baptized, and wash away thy sins, calling on the name of the Lord **(Acts 22:16)**.*

That God's word is incorporated onto a cell phone, how far will a phone sail, if it is powered up through the word of God? Furthermore, how far will God take us, through a cell phone, for the call He has on our lives?

> *But Jesus beheld them, and said unto them, With men this is impossible; but with God all things are possible **(Matthew 19:26)**. And ye are complete in him, which is the head of all principality and power: In whom also ye are circumcised with the circumcision made without hands, in putting off the body of the sins of the flesh by the circumcision of Christ: Buried with him in baptism, wherein also ye are risen with him through the faith of the operation of God, who hath raised him from the dead **(Colossians 2:10-12)**.*

"Any Great Memories Of Life You Wish To Repeat?"

There are times that we have great moments in a day. But, it's funny how a person would say, "I wish that I could live this day again!" If you had a day that went so well, where you would wish to repeat it, then you will have to give back everything of that great moment, that you received, to start over.

Brethren, I count not myself to have apprehended: but this one thing I do, forgetting those things which are behind, and reaching forth unto those things which are before, I press toward the mark for the prize of the high calling of God in Christ Jesus **(Philippians 3:13-14)**.

Why give back what you are so grateful for, to receive your same blessing twice? Will it reflect upon your heart the second time around, as it did when you accepted your blessing for the first time? On that note, if every present time in which you live in, is a gift from God, will God give you the same gift twice, in a different present moment? You will already be aware of what you are receiving. Furthermore, if your mind is a gift from God, and you received the same gift twice, would you have felt better if you were double-minded? If a single thought crossed your mind, that made you feel good, then how much better would you have felt, if that same thought came to you twice, as a double-cross?

If a person is double-minded, then it may cause that person to be two-faced.

A double minded man is unstable in all his ways *(James 1:8)*.

Moreover, if you were double-sighted, wouldn't you see a $100 bill as two $100 bills? Perhaps, by the look of things, and the feel of things, it would convey two different levels of statements. Your mind's eye would have stated, "I have two Benjamin Franklins."

"Looking at two $100 bills from a double-sighted viewpoint"

But, by the feel of things, you only have one Benjamin Franklin." Your statement will not come back void.

If eyeglasses will help your vision, will that make you feel better in knowing your true currency, or would you rather go back to your current double-sighted untruths, and overreact, feeling double-crossed?

There are many situations in life, where you can't only go by the looks of things, but you have to make choices by the feel of things. That's when the Holy Spirit gives you discernment, by feeling from your heart.

> *While we look not at the things which are seen, but at the things which are not seen: for the things which are seen are temporal; but the things which are not seen are eternal **(2 Corinthians 4:18)**. And I will pray the Father, and he shall give you another Comforter, that he may abide with you for ever; Even the Spirit of truth; whom the world cannot receive, because it seeth him not, neither knoweth him: but ye know him; for he dwelleth with you, and shall be in you **(John 14:16-17)**.*

Moreover, if being double-sighted or double-minded is not a good thing to have, doesn't mean that you should not have a double vision. To have a double vision can also signify having a "Plan A" and "Plan B".

> *Remember ye not the former things, neither consider the things of old **(Isaiah 43:18)**. And be not conformed to this world: but be ye transformed by the*

*renewing of your mind, that ye may prove what is that good, and acceptable, and perfect, will of God (**Romans 12:2**). Whereas ye know not what shall be on the morrow. For what is your life? It is even a vapour, that appeareth for a little time, and then vanisheth away (**James 4:14**). For whatsoever things were written aforetime were written for our learning, that we through patience and comfort of the scriptures might have hope (**Romans 15:4**).*

Do you like taking tests? If a test went great for you, do you wish to take that same test again, just for the fun of it, or would you rather move on to something else? If everyday that you go through is a test of your faith, and your current day is going so well, then why repeat a day, where your faith may not pass the test the second time around? A test may have the same questions and answers, but if you repeat a day for the second time, where everyone else have moved on with their lives, then you will encounter new faces with new experiences and challenges. The solutions to the same problems may take on a more complicated approach. If there are new experiences that you will have to face, then the choices that you make may cause confusion on that synonymous test. If you are wishing to repeat a day again, and your blessings have a date on them, then why turn back time to prolong your awaited blessings?

*Then goeth he, and taketh with himself seven other spirits more wicked than himself, and they enter in and dwell there: and the last state of that man is worse than the first. Even so shall it be also unto this wicked generation (**Matthew 12:45**). A man's heart deviseth his way: but the LORD directeth his steps (**Proverbs 16:9**). For I know the thoughts that I think toward you, says the LORD, thoughts of peace and not of evil,* *to give you a future and a hope **(Jeremiah 29:11 NKJV)**. Boast not thyself of to morrow; for thou knowest not what a day may bring forth **(Proverbs 27:1)**.*

God is the power source as Wi-Fi connects to the signal. The word, through Jesus Christ, is the password to your blessings that comes in time, through the Lord's perfect data. But, if we refuse to move on from a good day or a bad day, then the programming of the data for our time frame would hold back our blessings. Moreover, if we stick to God's program, through His power, our data would line up with the blessings that He promised us.

*In the beginning was the Word, and the Word was with God, and the Word was God. The same was in the beginning with God. All things were made by him; and without him was not any thing made that was made. In him was life; and the life was the light of men **(John 1:1-4)**. For I am not ashamed of the gospel of Christ: for it is the power of God unto salvation to every one that believeth; to the Jew first, and also to the Greek **(Romans 1:16)**. The law of the LORD is perfect, converting the soul: the testimony of the LORD is sure, making wise the simple **(Psalm 19:7)**. And it shall come to pass, if thou shalt hearken diligently unto the voice of the LORD thy God, to observe and to do all his commandments which I command thee this day, that the LORD thy God will set thee on high above all nations of the earth: And all these blessings shall come on thee, and overtake thee, if thou shalt hearken unto the voice of the LORD thy God **(Deuteronomy 28:1-2)**. Now unto him that is able to do exceeding abundantly above all that we ask or think, according to the power that worketh in us, Unto him be glory in the church by Christ Jesus throughout all ages, world without end. Amen **(Ephesians 3:20-21)**.*

"The Importance Of Your Livers and Heart"

There are times that we are stored in the wrong place, so we have to be restored, to see brighter beginnings. The liver and heart collaborate together, to ensure the blood circulates healthfully throughout the body. They both work together as a team.

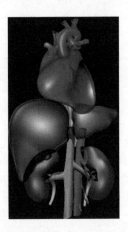

Physiologically, blood and bile intimately tie liver and heart health together:

1. Blood – The liver receives 25% of the blood driven by the heart and filters over two quarts of blood every minute. To ensure optimal circulation and filtration, the heart pumps blood while the liver purges it.

2. *Bile* – To dissolve fat in the blood vessels, the liver produces up to two cups of bile a day. Without bile, our arteries would be as hard as

rocks without any hope of circulating blood throughout the heart, liver or remainder of the body." (https://www.liversupport.com/the-link-between-liver-and-heart-disease/)

*And Jesus knowing their thoughts said, Wherefore think ye evil in your hearts (**Matthew 9:4**)? And he shall offer thereof his offering, even an offering made by fire unto the LORD; the fat that covereth the inwards, and all the fat that is upon the inwards, And the two kidneys, and the fat that is upon them, which is by the flanks, and the caul above the liver, with the kidneys, it shall he take away. And the priest shall burn them upon the altar: it is the food of the offering made by fire for a sweet savour: all the fat is the LORD's. It shall be a perpetual statute for your generations throughout all your dwellings, that ye eat neither fat nor blood (**Leviticus 3:14-17**).*

If eating livers are good for your eyes (www.firmoo.com/answer/question/11194.html), and your liver, in which you were created with, are placed close to your heart, then can your liver see your heart?

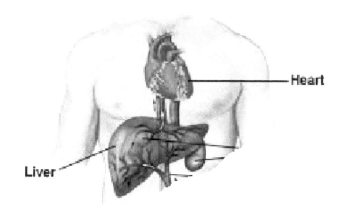

That eating livers are also good for your blood, there are times, that as a body of Christ, we will have to be delivered from our hearts, through the blood of Christ.

> *And he took the blind man by the hand, and led him out of the town; and when he had spit on his eyes, and put his hands upon him, he asked him if he saw ought. And he looked up, and said, I see men as trees, walking. After that he put his hands again upon his eyes, and made him look up: and he was restored, and saw every man clearly (**Mark 8:23-25**).*

Perhaps, that's why the thinking in our hearts causes pains to the closest elements to our hearts.

The thinking of our hearts may have our minds twisted.

Is that why many people get breast cancer, heart attaches, liver cancer, etc.?

> *Turn thee unto me, and have mercy upon me; for I am desolate and afflicted. The troubles of my heart are enlarged: O bring thou me out of my distresses. Look upon mine affliction and my pain; and forgive all my sins* **(Psalms 25:16-18)**.

Therefore, we have to be careful with what we do, say, react to, and listen to, because that, which draws us, will be our picture to every action that we make. It will also be the image for our lives.

IMAGE = PICTURE

That, which you would attend to, will stick to you, because you can't change what has already happened. Therefore, it will pen/pin to you. What pens to you, depends on your actions. A writing pen is a permanent mark that will stick to the written pages of your life story. On the other hand, a needle pin is a point that will stick to you as a mark of your life story. But, you can change the following phases of the outcome. How do you want the picture of your life to be drawn? Who do you choose to draw your blood, when you know that your blood is what gives you life? Moreover, if you don't live by God, the Liver who created you, then how can you see the light? Furthermore, if you don't live by your heart, then how can you live by the Liver/liver, that lives in you? Isn't the heart and the liver connected together? But, if your liver isn't right, then what god/good do you serve, if your heart is corrupt? If the liver and the heart were not closely connected, then how would you be a liver in Christ from the heart? Furthermore, if something came between the liver and the heart, then how would you live, if "HE" (The Father) does not "ART" through you?

"HE"-THE FATHER IS THE "ART" OF YOU. THEREFORE, LET GOD WORK IN THE HEART OF YOU!

> *Till a dart strike through his liver; as a bird hasteth to the snare, and knoweth not that it is for his life **(Proverbs 7:23)**. That ye put off concerning the former conversation the old man, which is corrupt according to the deceitful lusts; And be renewed in the spirit of your mind; And that ye put on the new man, which after God is created in righteousness and true holiness **(Ephesians 4:22-24)**.*

Moreover, if Jesus was delivered up to Heaven, after dying for our sins, then shouldn't we sacrifice being delivered through Christ? If we can be delivered through Christ, who strengthens us, then we can relive, or perhaps, we can be a re-liver, by being born again, to be a re-liver for eternal life.

> *Now ye are the body of Christ, and members in particular **(1 Corinthians 12:27)**. He that spared not his own Son, but delivered him up for us all, how shall he not with him also freely give us all things **(Romans 8:32)**?*

"100 Paths To Choose"

There are 100 paths, where 99 routes will lead you to eternal condemnation. If these 100 paths were a multiple choice question, and they were side by side, with all 100 doors open for you to choose, which path will you walk, the right path, one of the 98 paths in the middle, or the one that's left?

God's voice cannot be heard, and there are no clues to search for. There is no one else to turn to. You have to depend on yourself, and your walk, as your walk will determine your choice.

> *There is a way which seemeth right unto a man, but the end thereof are the ways of death* ***(Proverbs 14:12)***.

All 100 doors open with heat and clouds of smoke. The route that you have chosen, there's no way to see, but walls to hold onto will guide your walk.

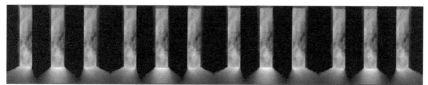

WHICH DOOR IS THE RIGHT PATH? IF YOU ARE FACED IN THE DIRECTION OF THE DOORS, THEN THE RIGHT PATH COULD BE ON THE SIDE THAT'S LEFT, AND THE SIDE THAT'S ON THE LEFT, MAY BE THE SIDE THAT'S RIGHT.

> *O LORD, I know that the way of man is not in himself: it is not in man that walketh to direct his steps*

(Jeremiah 10:23). Man's goings are of the LORD; how can a man then understand his own way (Proverbs 20:24)? And the smoke of their torment ascendeth up for ever and ever: and they have no rest day nor night, who worship the beast and his image, and whosoever receiveth the mark of his name (Revelation 14:11).

At this point, there are no stumbling blocks, as you continue to hope. As you abide in hope, one lane has a turn with many choices to get your journey right. The other 99 lanes have no choice. The walls continues to get hotter and hotter. The doors are locked, where there is no turning back.

"ALL THE DOORS ARE LOCKED!"

Out of 100 lanes to choose from, God has placed us in His lane, to strive for His destiny, where we will make mistakes, and have many turns ahead, to get our journey right.

What if there were 1,000 lanes for your multiple choice question? Which lane would be the correct route if 999 lanes were wrong? On that note, how long can each 9 stand the test, before it stumbles over to a 666?

Here is wisdom. Let him that hath understanding count the number of the beast: for it is the number of a man; and his number is Six hundred threescore and six (Revelation 13:18). There is no peace, saith the LORD, unto the wicked (Isaiah 48:22).

If you were trying out for a team, and one more error caused you to be disqualified from making the cut, then how careful would you be if that one more error causes you to be cut from the Lord's team?

In flaming fire taking vengeance on them that know not God, and that obey not the gospel of our Lord Jesus Christ: Who shall be punished with everlasting destruction from the presence of the Lord, and from the glory of his power **(2 Thessalonians 1:8-9)***; Enter ye in at the strait gate: for wide is the gate, and broad is the way, that leadeth to destruction, and many there be which go in thereat: Because strait is the gate, and narrow is the way, which leadeth unto life, and few there be that find it* **(Matthew 7:13-14)***.*

"Son-Of-A-Gun VS Son-Of-God"

It's something how people speak the term, "You son-of-a-gun" with exceeding joy. But, we very seldom speak in terms, "Son-of-God!" But, isn't a gun a deadly weapon, and "Son-of-God" a lively weapon, who gives us exceeding joy? Furthermore, why TRI-umph over a lethal weapon, when you can TRI God's legal weapon (The Word of God), and be safe?

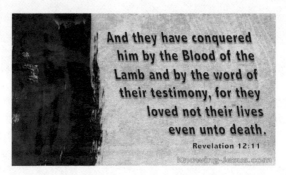

And they have conquered him by the Blood of the Lamb and by the word of their testimony, for they loved not their lives even unto death.

Revelation 12:11

knowing-Jesus.com

Moreover, doesn't God have power over any gun?

> *Behold, I have created the smith that bloweth the coals in the fire, and that bringeth forth an instrument for his work; and I have created the waster to destroy. No weapon that is formed against thee shall prosper; and every tongue that shall rise against thee in judgment thou shalt condemn. This is the heritage of the servants of the LORD, and their righteousness is of me, saith the LORD* **(Isaiah 54:16-17)**.

Would you rather shoot a gun, or give a shout to God? With a gun that's made of man, you have the power in your hand to make a straight shot. But, with God, who made man, will give you power over all weapons that are formed against you. If you give a shout to God, He will keep you straight on target.

> *As newborn babes, desire the sincere milk of the word, that ye may grow thereby: If so be ye have tasted that the Lord is gracious. To whom coming, as unto a living stone, disallowed indeed of men, but chosen of God, and precious, Ye also, as lively stones, are built up a spiritual house, an holy priesthood, to offer up spiritual sacrifices, acceptable to God by Jesus Christ. Wherefore also it is contained in scripture, BEHOLD, I LAY IN SION A CHIEF CORNER STONE, ELECT, PRECIOUS: AND HE THAT BELIEVETH ON HIM SHALL NOT BE CONFOUNDED. Unto you therefore which believe he is precious: but unto them which be disobedient, THE STONE WHICH THE BUILDERS DISALLOWED, THE SAME IS MADE THE HEAD OF THE CORNER (1 Peter 2:2-7),*

If you can literally stick a gun inside the volume of a bible, being that the bible is not condensed in size, then wouldn't the word of the Lord give coverage to a 38 magnum?

If that is the case in which it can hold that weapon, then why trust in something that's smaller than the word of God, to have protection over your life? A bible can fit into your hand, and you can carry it around in a case, everywhere you go. But, if you take page by page of the wisdom of God, and build on that, wouldn't His word cover you as a tent?

I TAKE MY SHELTER IN YOU.
Psalm 143:9

Furthermore, if you can place a gun inside the bible, then whose volume is the loudest, that will give you the most fear?

> *And fear not them which kill the body, but are not able to kill the soul: but rather fear him which is able to destroy both soul and body in hell (Matthew 10:28).*

Moreover, would you rather approach the son of someone pointing a gun at your head, or would you prefer to approach the Son-of-God, to make Him your head, to point you in the right direction, from all harm?

> *And who is he that will harm you, if ye be followers of that which is good (1 Peter 3:13)?*

A son-of-a-gun may miss the point, and target someone else's blood to take their life. The point in which they were directed, by their main/man head leader was misunderstood and they took the wrong blood. But, with the Son-of-God, Jesus' blood hits right on point, and targets to save your life. Furthermore, would you rather have a gun drawn for your blood, or would you prefer Jesus' blood drawn, in written formation, to guide you through life?

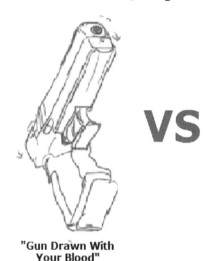

VS

ST. JOHN, 4   *The miss*

should not perish, but have eternal life.
16 ¶ For "God so loved the world, that he gave his only begotten Son, that whosoever believeth in him should not perish, but have everlasting life.
17 For "God sent not his Son into the world to condemn the world; but that the world through him might be saved.
18 ¶ He that believeth on him 'is not condemned: but he that believeth not is condemned already, because he hath not believed in the name of the only begotten Son of God.
19 And this is the condemnation, that 'light is come into the world, and men loved darkness rather than light, because their deeds were evil.
20 For every one that doeth evil hateth the light, neither cometh to the light, lest his deeds should be 'reproved.
21 But he that doeth truth cometh to the light, that his deeds may be made manifest, that they are wrought in God.

"Gun Drawn With Your Blood"   "Jesus' Blood Written For Your Life"

"A LETHAL WEAPON CAUSES STRIFE, BUT THE WORD OF GOD GIVES YOU LIFE!"

God made man. Therefore, He has control over man. That a gun is made by man, a man has jurisdiction over a gun. Therefore, why put your trust in something that you have power over, instead of putting your trust in God, who created you under His power? If you had a choice to be with a son-of-a-gun or the Son-Of-God, whose sentence would you rather be covered in for life?

*But we had the sentences of death in ourselves, that
we should not trust in ourselves, but in God which
raiseth the dead: Who delivered us from so great a
death, and doth deliver: in whom we trust that he will
yet deliver us (2 Corinthians 1:9-10);*

Moreover, whose tent/tense are you under? Why not
trust in God to give you a twist of English to your life
story by your faith in Him?

*Then a cloud covered the tent of the congregation, and
the glory of the LORD filled the tabernacle
(Exodus 40:34).*

THERE ARE 3 MAIN VERB TENSE/TENTS:

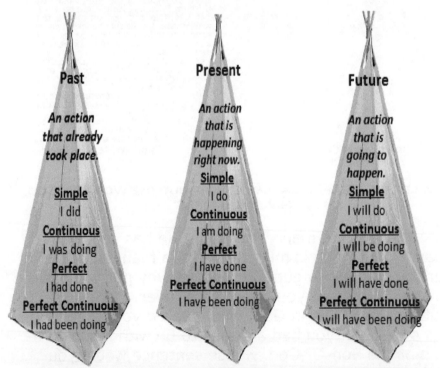

Past

An action
that already
took place.

Simple
I did
Continuous
I was doing
Perfect
I had done
Perfect Continuous
I had been doing

Present

An action
that is
happening
right now.
Simple
I do
Continuous
I am doing
Perfect
I have done
Perfect Continuous
I have been doing

Future

An action
that is
going to
happen.
Simple
I will do
Continuous
I will be doing
Perfect
I will have done
Perfect Continuous
I will have been doing

IF YOU WERE TWISTED BY YOUR PAST, THEN HOW WOULD YOU
PRESENT YOURSELF IN THE NOW, TO PREDICT YOUR FUTURE?

What skeletons are in your closet? Furthermore, what skeletons are in your tents/tense? In other words, do you ponder over memories of the *past*, or do you focus on the *present* to predict your *future*? Perhaps, if you focus on the *present*, the gift will come to you. What tent/tense are you sentenced under for life? If you are in the *past* tense/tent, what you had should stay in the past in order for you to pass the test, and not tense up on bad memories. If you are in the *future* tense/tent, what you will have, is for you to have at God's will. If you are in the *present* tense/tent, the moment that you are having now, is a present for every moment that you are alive. It will affect your *future* for every tense/tenth of a second. After all is said, would you rather be sentenced as a prisoner to life for the Son of God, or sentenced for life as a prisoner for being with a son of a gun?

> Now unto him that is able to keep you from falling, and to present you faultless before the presence of his glory with exceeding joy. To the only wise God our Saviour, be glory and majesty, dominion and power, both now and ever. A-men' *(Jude 1:24-25)*.

"From Funny Money To Rich Wisdom"

I approached a man one afternoon, as he was going into the trunk of his car.

I said: Hello Sir! Do you support entrepreneurs that are working toward a positive cause?

He replied: Yes, I do, at times when I can. What do you have?

I stated: I wrote a book.

He replied: Really? What is your book about?

I let him browse through the book, and I shared one of my examples with him.

He said: I really like that example. That's a great "Food For Thought". Ahhh man, I wish that I could purchase your book, but right now, my money's funny!

I replied: Really Sir? You know what? The jokes in my book are funny too. Why not do a trade for a trade? Wait a minute. Before we do that, you said that your money is funny? That doesn't make it counterfeit does it?

He said: No, it doesn't make it counterfeit (As he
    laughs).

I replied: I tell you what, I'll trade you the funny book
    for the funny money. Since your money's
    so funny, I'll laugh it right to the bank,
    deposit it, and change it from funny to
    funding, and guess what?

He said: What?

I replied: The deposit won't take the fun out of it.

He said: Ahhh man, I never heard it like that before.

I replied: Me neither sir. The Lord just gave it to me
    like that.

Even though he didn't purchase my book with his
funny money, I'm sure that I left him with something
to think about.

I've heard the expression, "Time is money!" If your currency may depreciate over time, then how do you speak about your wealth at the current time of depreciation? Do you speak positive energy or negative energy? Perhaps, if you speak negative about your cash flow, then you are speaking depreciation into your bank account.

> But I say unto you, That every idle word that men shall speak, they shall give account thereof in the day of judgment. For by thy words thou shalt be justified, and by thy words thou shalt be condemned **(Matthew 12:36-37)**.

It's hilarious how someone would say, "Put your money where your mouth is!" If a person makes this statement, to bet another man's/woman's money, means that they disagree with what comes out of their mouth, for it to be a negative. Therefore, if you disapprove of what comes out of another person's mouth, and you won the bet, then why take someone else's money where their mouth has been?

"PUT YOUR MONEY WHERE YOUR MOUTH IS"

Perhaps, you will walk around with a contagious disagreement, or an infectious negative agreement until you get rid of the liquid assets.

"LIQUID ASSETS DRIPPING AWAY"

Furthermore, why would you walk around with the proceeds from someone's mouth who is all talk, but no truth, and whom you never believed in the first place, for the reason that you bet them? Their proceeds will rub off on you. Perhaps, you will walk around with their false belief, or doubt. Then, how can you proceed in life for yourself by faith, if you gain the proceeds of someone else, whom you have no trust? Maybe their proceeds would come out counterfeit. If so, then you will have an added fit to your worries. Moreover, that false money is bad business, then their liquid assets will turn your business into a liquidation.

> *Set a watch, O LORD, before my mouth; keep the door of my lips **(Psalm 141:3)**. He that hath knowledge spareth his words: and a man of understanding is of an excellent spirit **(Proverbs 17:27)**. He becometh poor*

that dealeth with a slack hand: but the hand of the diligent maketh rich **(Proverbs 10:4)**. *Let no corrupt communication proceed out of your mouth, but that which is good to the use of edifying, that it may minister grace unto the hearers* **(Ephesians 4:29)**.

I've heard the term, "Money talks!"

$MONEY TALKS$

If you put your money in a check, then doesn't it give you a financial statement? But, our mouths also make statements. There are times that we have to put ourselves in check, by the words that we speak.

DO YOU PUT YOURSELF IN CHECK?

Either make the tree good, and his fruit good; or else make the tree corrupt, and his fruit corrupt: for the tree is known by his fruit. O generation of vipers, how can ye, being evil, speak good things? for out of the abundance of the heart the mouth speaketh. A good man out of the good treasure of the heart bringeth forth good things: and an evil man out of the evil treasure bringeth forth evil things
(Matthew 12:33-35).

Therefore, if you tell someone to put their money where their mouth is, and you won the bet, why take money from a person, whose word of mouth is incorrect, for their statements to come back void? How can you bank on them? If you put your money with a trust account, then the bank will serve as a custodian, and a trustee will keep legal control of the proceeds in the account. The trustee can be an accountant, a lawyer, or a family member to take over someone else's assets to handle the funds, and the payments better, such as property cost. Therefore, why would you bank on a bet that you may win, and take money from a mouth that you have no trust? Perhaps, you would walk away having a bad fit. But, if the statements that comes out from the person's mouth is not real, then you may walk away with a counterfeit. If that's the case, you will walk around with funny money that can't be replaced. Then, you may intend to counteract.

Labour not to be rich: cease from thine own wisdom. Wilt thou set thine eyes upon that which is not? for riches certainly make themselves wings; they fly away as an eagle toward heaven **(Proverbs 23:4-5)**.

Isn't it amazing how the words that we speak, may change our lives? Let's look at the power of words from an algebraic perspective. As I will take the number two (2), and times (X) it to the 3rd power, I will retrieve this result:

$$2^3 = 2 \times 2 \times 2$$
$$= 4 \times 2$$
$$= 8$$

Now, with this same number (2), I will use the "word power" in the place of the "3rd power". As there are four different letters in "word", I will employ the least whole number power for each letter. Therefore, w=1, o=2, r=3, and d=4.

2 TO THE "WORD" POWER IS WRITTEN AS: 2ᵂᴼᴿᴰ

Now, multiple each letter of "word" by replacing them with their respective numbers:

W X O X R X D =

1 X 2 X 3 X 4 = 24

Therefore, giving you 2 to the 24th power, written as:

$$2^{24} = 16{,}777{,}216$$

Wow! This is taking a small number, as a mustard seed, and using the power of a positive word, to grow the mustard seed into a harvest.

It is like a grain of mustard seed, which, when it is sown in the earth, is less than all the seeds that be in *the earth: But when it is sown, it groweth up, and becometh greater than all herbs, and shooteth out great branches; so that the fowls of the air may lodge under the shadow of it **(Mark 4:31-32)**.*

Perhaps, you've heard the phrase, "One bad apple spoils the bunch!" Of all the positive letters in "word", if one of the members are negative, it will spoil it for the bunch. I will incorporate the least powered letter (w), to make it a negative one (-1), while the other letters will stay positive. As I bring up the same equation, I arrive to:

$$W=-1, O=2, R=3, \text{ AND } D=4$$

$$2^{WORD} = 2^{(-1 \times 2 \times 3 \times 4)}$$
$$= 2^{-24}$$

$$= \frac{1}{16,777,216}.$$

It looks like, by the aftermath of the problem, from that one negative, or that negative one, everything that was built up over time, hide under the table. Isn't it something how one negative power seed can spoil it for the harvest? That's why we have to be careful with what we speak, and choose our words wisely. A negative reward is by a negative drawer. Therefore, if you speak negatively, then you will draw negative, and receive negative.

REWARD IS DRAWER SPELLED BACKWARDS

*Your glorying is not good. Know ye not that a little leaven leaveneth the whole lump? Purge out therefore the old leaven, that ye may be a new lump, as ye are unleavened. For even Christ our passover is sacrificed for us: Therefore let us keep the feast, not with old leaven, neither with the leaven of malice and wickedness; but with the unleavened bread of sincerity and truth **(1 Corinthians 5:6-8)**.*

As words have power, then what power have you given money to move from you? Furthermore, do you budget your money, or does your money budge from you?

*Let your conversation be without covetousness; and be content with such things as ye have: for he hath said, I WILL NEVER LEAVE THEE, NOR FORSAKE THEE **(Hebrews 13:5)**. For the love of money is the root of all evil: which while some coveted after, they have erred from the faith, and pierced themselves through with many sorrows. But thou, O man of God, flee these things; and follow after righteousness, godliness, faith, love, patience, meekness **(1 Timothy 6:10-11)**.*

That words are rich, then how valuable is each letter? If letters can merge together to form a word of power, then what strength do you have in a power statement. Moreover, if words can come together to make a statement with power, then how much more power will we have, if we come 2 or 3 gathered together, in agreement, through prayer? A prayer can build to structure paragraphs/pair-of-graphs. Therefore, paragraphs/pair-of-graphs can draw pictures, and each picture is worth a thousand words.

> *Again I say unto you, That if two of you shall agree on earth as touching any thing that they shall ask, it shall be done for them of my Father which is in heaven. For where two or three are gathered together in my name, there am I in the midst of them* **(Matthew 18:19-20)**.

"Get Tried By The Lord"

When you are transformed from this world, are you then tri-formed from this world? "Tri" means three, and "Three" stands for trinity. Trinity stands for "Father + Son + Holy Ghost". You have to "Tri/try all 3 together to experience their will for your existence. If you are not tried by the Lord, then how can you be equipped for His will in your life, to be transformed from glory to glory? Moreover, if you don't go by the Lord's will/wheel, then how can you be well rounded, and go in the right path?

> *And be not conformed to this world: but be ye transformed by the renewing of your mind, that ye may prove what is that good, and acceptable, and perfect, will of God **(Romans 12:2)**. Go ye therefore, and teach all nations, baptizing them in the name of the Father, and of the Son, and of the Holy Ghost **(Matthew 28:19)**: Now the Lord is that Spirit: and where the Spirit of the Lord is, there is liberty. But we all, with open Face beholding as in a glass the glory of the Lord, are changed into the same image from glory to glory, even as by the Spirit of the Lord **(2 Corinthians 3:17-18)**. The angel of the LORD encampeth round about them that fear him, and delivereth them. O taste and see that the LORD is good: blessed is the man that trusteth in him **(Psalms 34:7-8)**.*

Let's look at "Tri" from a different angle. The word "Trigon" is another word for triangle. If we don't go by the angle of God, then we have "Gon" (gone) astray, instead of going in the right angle. Perhaps, we will be tri-aled in judgment. In elaborating on "Gon", it is used in many forms:

- It is a verb, used as a present participle of "go".

- "-gon" is a suffix defined as a shape having a specified number of angles.

- "gon-" is a prefix defined as a variant of gono-.

If we do not meditate on God's word, to know His instruction for our lives, then we have "-gon"/gone a different way. If we go in the way of the Lord, then we will know the angle that He's coming from. Neither one of us are perfect, but if we go by the Lord's angle, then we can be in the midst of His will/wheel.

> *I will meditate in thy precepts, and have respect unto thy ways* **(Psalm 119:15)**. *Thou wilt keep him in perfect peace, whose mind is stayed on thee: because he trusteth in thee* **(Isaiah 26:3)**.

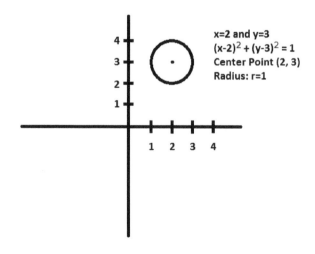

Furthermore, wouldn't you rather be in the tire of the Lord, to roll with His will/wheel, than to be tired of man's will/wheel sloping you in the wrong direction?

> *There is a way which seemeth right unto a man, but the end thereof are the ways of death* **(Proverbs 14:12)**.

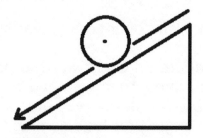

Perhaps, you will have to retire from one will/wheel to roll/role with another. If you don't roll/role with God, how would you act? Moreover, if you act on man's will/wheel, to roll/role with him, then how would you get played in the act? Even when man retires for that day, he's under a lot of pressure from a screw up.

Man under pressure to screw up his wheel, as he retires.

On the other hand, when you act in a role for a play, aren't you trying to be like someone else? That's why God gives us a vision, to see where we're at, by Him. God's will/wheel for our lives never changes. It is still the same from beginning to end. Therefore, God never retires from His plan, in our lives. Furthermore, if you are under the will/wheel of man without tools, to make your drive stronger, then how far would you go down the road of life, before you realize that you aren't moving up?

> *Every good gift and every perfect gift is from above, and cometh down from the Father of lights, with whom is no variableness, neither shadow of turning **(James 1:17)**. For I am the Lord, I change not; therefore ye sons of Jacob are not consumed **(Malachi 3:6)**. Let every soul be subject unto the higher powers. For there is no power but of God: the powers that be are ordained of God **(Romans 13:1)**.*

The Lord's angle is up, and to the right. That's why we are always at the right hand of God.

> *Therefore being by the right hand of God exalted, and having received of the Father the promise of the Holy Ghost, he hath shed forth this, which ye now see and hear **(Acts 2:33)**.*

If we are not upright with the Lord, then how can you be the center point of His will/wheel, where the x-axis and the y-axis are both in the positive? Moreover, God wants us to be straight up and straight forward with Him, because He supplies the right tools to give us drive.

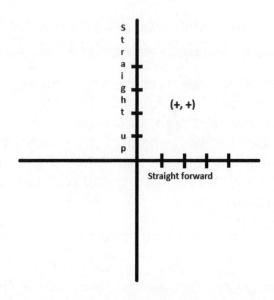

*And they went every one straight forward: whither
the spirit was to go, they went; and they turned not
when they went (Ezekiel 1:12). Now as I beheld the
living creatures, behold one wheel upon the earth by
the living creatures, with his four faces. The
appearance of the wheels and their work was like unto
the colour of a beryl: and they four had one likeness:
and their appearance and their work was as it were a
wheel in the middle of a wheel (Ezekiel 1:15-16). For
the LORD God is a sun and shield: the LORD will give
grace and glory: no good thing will he withhold from
them that walk uprightly (Psalm 84:11). Thou hast
also given me the shield of thy salvation: and thy right
hand hath holden me up, and thy gentleness hath
made me great (Psalm 18:35).*

It's amazing, that by man's algebraic
expressions, all 4 angles of the x and y axis are right
angles. But, how can they all be right, or how can
they be alright if the other three angles are in line
with negative?

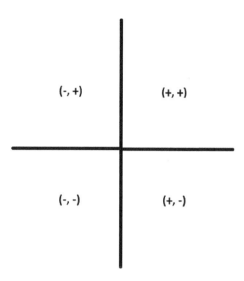

Isn't it interesting, with the times (X) of men or women being in the negative, they are accounted for as positive? Even against all odds:

$$\textbf{-3 X -5 = +15}$$

> *Recompense to no man evil for evil. Provide things honest in the sight of all men. If it be possible, as much as lieth in you, live peaceably with all men. Dearly beloved, avenge not yourselves, but rather give place unto wrath: for it is written, VENGEANCE IS MINE; I WILL REPAY, saith the Lord. Therefore IF THINE ENEMY HUNGER, FEED HIM; IF HE THIRST, GIVE HIM DRINK: FOR IN SO DOING THOU SHALT HEAP COALS OF FIRE ON HIS HEAD. Be not overcome of evil, but overcome evil with good* **(Romans 12:17-21)**.

It's funny how many people want to follow the footsteps of man, because he looks like he's been walking the right path. Looks can be deceiving. Can you imagine that when people are asked, "Where did you go to just now?" Even the most profound leaders may gladly say, "I just went down the block." And you still want to follow them? But, why follow the steps of man who have walked down the block, when you can follow the steps of God, who will raise you up, and has no blocks to down you, for your path, or your walk of life through Him?

WALKING IN MAN'S FOOTSTEPS IS A DANGEROUS PATH TO WALK.

*O LORD, I know that the way of man is not in himself: it is not in man that walketh to direct his steps **(Jeremiah 10:23)**. There is a way that seemeth right unto a man; but the end thereof are the ways of death **(Proverbs 16:25)**. The steps of a good man are ordered by the LORD: and he delighteth in his way **(Psalm 37:23)**. For even hereunto were ye called: because Christ also suffered for us, leaving us an example, that ye should follow his steps **(1 Peter 2:21)**: Enter not into the path of the wicked, and go not in the way of evil men **(Proverbs 4:14)**.*

Therefore, why listen to man's report? Instead, adhere/add hear/add ear to God's report. Man's angles of life are not always positive, because they don't always add up with a cross (+) examination. But, the Lord's angle, for our lives, is always positive, and positive in all ways. Jesus crisscrossed/Christ-crossed for our lives. Moreover, that Jesus died for our sins, isn't that a plus (+)? You do the math.

JESUS CROSS MULTIPLYING (X) FOR OUR LIVES IS ALSO A PLUS (+). THAT JESUS IS 2ND, AFTER GOD, WHO IS 1ST, IS THAT WHY: 2 X 2 = 4, AND 2 + 2 = 4? WHEN JESUS CROSS MULTIPLY, HE ADDS UP TO THE SAME!

> *My son, attend to my words; incline thine ear unto my sayings. Let them not depart from thine eyes; keep them in the midst of thine heart. For they are life unto those that find them, and health to all their flesh* **(Proverbs 4:20-22)**. *For Christ also hath once suffered for sins, the just for the unjust, that he might bring us to God, being put to death in the flesh, but quickened by the Spirit* **(1 Peter 3:18)**:

"A Kodak Moment vs A Show That-Moment"

It has been said, "A picture is worth a thousand words." On the contrary, it has also been said, "Actions speaks louder than words." But, do actions speak louder words?

- A Kodak moment is a picture taken.

- A show is a picture in action.

If a picture is worth a thousand words, then I wonder how many words can you summarize through your actions? If you go to the movies to see a picture in action, how will that picture move you? Then, after what you've learned, how would you act? With that being said, do your thoughts keep you in bondage?

*For ye have not received the spirit of bondage again to fear; but ye have received the Spirit of adoption, whereby we cry, Ab'-ba, Father **(Romans 8:15)**. And deliver them who through fear of death were all their lifetime subject to bondage **(Hebrews 2:15)**.*

If the thoughts of your mind were caught on camera, how many sentences will you have in your story?

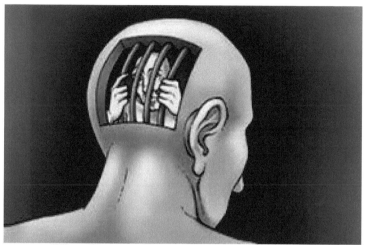

"THE PRISON SENTENCE OF HIS MIND"

Moreover, how many sentences would you have in a lifetime? Furthermore, if the thinking of a person's mind were to be captured on film, how many stories would there be in each prison, and how many life sentences would be on each story? If you were a judge that made one mistake in a sentence to a paragraph, that error may cause a person a life sentence in prison, that have only taken you a few minutes to write/right. But instead, you would have wronged them through a trial and error.

> *Speak not evil one of another, brethren. He that speaketh evil of his brother, and judgeth his brother, speaketh evil of the law: but if thou judge the law, thou art not a doer of the law, but a judge. There is one lawgiver, who is able to save and to destroy: who art thou that judgest another (**James 4:11-12**)?*

Words are powerful, as you have to not only watch what you speak, but you have to, also, be careful with what you speak,

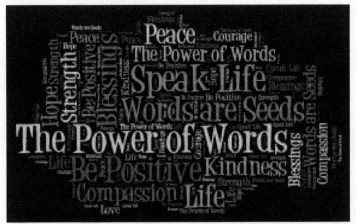

"IF YOU CAN'T WATCH WHAT YOU SPEAK, THEN CAN YOU REALLY SEE WHAT YOU'RE SAYING YOURSELF? IF NOT, THEN YOU ARE BLIND TO YOUR OWN WORDS."

because a sentence and a statement can work hand and hand. If you say or give the wrong statement, isn't it amazing how that may cause you to be sentenced? On the flip side, if you said the wrong sentence, then the statement in which you bank on, may come back void.

> *For the word of God is quick, and powerful, and sharper than any twoedged sword, piercing even to the dividing asunder of soul and spirit, and of the joints and marrow, and is a discerner of the thoughts and intents of the heart* **(Hebrews 4:12)**. *For HE THAT WILL LOVE LIFE, AND SEE GOOD DAYS, LET HIM REFRAIN HIS TONGUE FROM EVIL, AND HIS LIPS THAT THEY SPEAK NO GUILE* **(1 Peter 3:10)**:

If you were sentenced for life, then what state of mind were you in, and to speak on the power of words, what statement got you there? If you are freed from the prison of your mind, then you can make state-of-the-art decisions. Moreover, can you Art like The Lord? Perhaps, you can draw freehanded. But, how can you make a great statement for yourself, if you are in another state of mind, other than your own? If you are in the sentence of another person's story, then how were you sent/sentenced there? The life of someone's story can be the prison of another person's mind.

But, why would someone sit on another person's sentence if they can make a statement for themselves to empower their lives?

> But be ye doers of the word, and not hearers only, deceiving your own selves *(James 1:22)*. Even so faith, if it hath not works, is dead, being alone *(James 2:17)*.

A Kodak moment is a picture taken at a particular time, but that photo may paint the wrong image to another person's mind. Where a "Show-That-Moment" is a moving picture on film, of a person's life, or a make believe story shown on stage, in action. It is obvious, in this passage, actions speak louder than words. Now, in looking from a different perspective, lets take a cat walking behind you, during the moment you were writing about "The Cat's Silent Foot Steps". The sound of the words being written on paper will be louder than the actions of the roaming cat. Perhaps, that's because your writings is your voice.

A Kodak moment is a flash shot, and a show-that-moment can be a flashback of memories.

FLASH SHOT   **FLASHBACK**

Would you rather have a flashback of your life, or a flash shot to new beginnings? A flashback will take you to the past, but to have a shot in life, will give you the opportunity to flash as a star/Starr, to reach others, and help them shine.

> *Let your light so shine before men, that they may see your good works, and glorify your Father which is in heaven* **(Matthew 5:16)**.

Perhaps, you can be their flashlight, to help them see the way.

The right way may not always be the easy way, but there are times that you will have to go through an experience in life, in order to prepare you for your blessings of new beginnings.

> *For the LORD knoweth the way of the righteous: but the way of the ungodly shall perish* ***(Psalm 1:6)***. *For our light affliction, which is but for a moment, worketh for us a far more exceeding and eternal weight of glory; While we look not at the things which are seen, but at the things which are not seen: for the things which are seen are temporal; but the things which are not seen are eternal* ***(2 Corinthians 4:17-18)***.

That's why you give thanks to the Lord in the process of going through, to know that your reward is soon to come. The Kodak moment of your blessing is your shot to share your testimony with others, so that you may flash and shine on others, to give them hope. The experiences that you suffer through, in your journey, will not compare to the blessings that will unfold for your life.

> *For I reckon that the sufferings of this present time are not worthy to be compared with the glory which shall be revealed in us* ***(Romans 8:18)***.

"Are You No Earthly Good Or All Heart"

God is the creator of Earth, but not the ruler over Earth.

> *In the beginning God created the heaven and the earth (**Genesis 1:1**).*

Satan is behind the works of Earth.

Earth — Eart(hell)

> *He that committeth sin is of the devil; for the devil sinneth from the beginning. For this purpose the Son of God was manifested, that he might destroy the works of the devil (**1 John 3:8**).*

That's why we, as Christians, are not of this world. Because God is the Ruler of the Heart, that's where He Arts. Through the Heart, we have an ear to hear, and we also have a heart to hear.

H*EAR*T

> *The king's heart is in the hand of the LORD, as the rivers of water: he turneth it whithersoever he will. Every way of a man is right in his own eyes: but the LORD pondereth the hearts (**Proverbs 21:1-2**).*

But, do people hear what they want to hear? If what you hear is in your heart, then what is said to the heart of your ears to control your actions?

> *Wherefore, my beloved brethren, let every man be swift to hear, slow to speak, slow to wrath: For the wrath of man worketh not the righteousness of God. Wherefore lay apart all filthiness and superfluity of naughtiness, and receive with meekness the engrafted word, which is able to save your souls* ***(James 1:19-21)***.

It's amazing how we all have a heartbeat followed by eardrums.

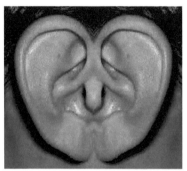

"WE HAVE TO BE CAREFUL WHAT WE LISTEN TO, BECAUSE IT INFORMS/FORMS THE HEART."

> *Also take no heed unto all words that are spoken; lest thou hear thy servant curse thee* ***(Ecclesiastes 7:21)***:

But, what do you hear in your heart? We are in the earth, but not of the earth. That's why we have to walk by faith, as the Lord guides our hearts. Just because we have a heartbeat, doesn't mean that the heart looses, but there are times that we have to get loosened from bondage, so we have to forgive what we hear from the heart, and not only what we hear from the ear. Perhaps, does the ear forget what's heard, before the heart forgives what's been heard? When we forgive people in a heartbeat, the Lord will turn our situation around to a heart-winner.

But love ye your enemies, and do good, and lend, hoping for nothing again; and your reward shall be great, and ye shall be the children of the Highest: for he is kind unto the unthankful and to the evil **(Luke 6:35)**.

Is it by what we hear that determines our/hour growth or fear? But, if we don't buy into it, then we won't loose it, and neither would it cost us?

Do you live on Earth by letting God of Heaven guide your way?

HEAVEN(EART) = H(EART)
= HEART
= HE ART

...or do you listen to the god whose behind this world (Satan), to tell/tale/tail you astray?

And let the peace of God rule in your hearts, to the which also ye are called in one body; and be ye thankful **(Colossians 3:15)**. *Howbeit when he, the Spirit of truth, is come, he will guide you into all truth: for he shall not speak of himself; but whatsoever he shall hear, that shall he speak: and he will shew you things to come* **(John 16:13)**.

It is hell who's all behind Earth.

EART(H) = EART(HELL)

*And the great dragon was cast out, that old serpent,
called the Devil, and Satan, which deceiveth the whole
world: he was cast out into the earth, and his angels
were cast out with him **(Revelation 12:9)**.*

On that note, where do you put your trust?

**"DO YOU LOVE PEOPLE TO DEATH, OR
DO YOU LOVE PEOPLE TO CHRIST/LIFE?"**

Do you bank on God's trust, or do you account with
"Hell", on Earth, only to give you an underpayment
penalty for eternal life? If you bank with a teller of
God, you will have true statements with the highest
return rates of interest, because we are all of God's
interest. But, if you trust with a teller of hell, your
statements will return void, and may turn into a
sentence for life in prison, with a stolen account.

*Put not your trust in princes, nor in the son of man, in whom there is no help. His breath goeth forth, he returneth to his earth; in that very day his thoughts perish. Happy is he that hath the God of Jacob for his help, whose hope is in the LORD his God **(Psalms 146:3-5)**:*

"WHAT TELL/TALE ARE THEY TRYING TO COVER-UP IN A STATEMENT?"

*If therefore ye have not been faithful in the unrighteous mammon, who will commit to your trust the true riches **(Luke 16:11)**?*

"Let God Be Your Ruler"

If God is The Ruler of our path, then we should not be re-lured by the path of man, going in many wrong directions. That God is Ruler, then man re-lures.

Re-lur (relure) is ruler spelled backwards.

The definition of lure: to tempt someone to do something.

Wouldn't you rather be led the right way, by The Ruler the first time, than to be re-lured down the wrong path, two or more times?

*Thy word is a lamp unto my feet, and a light unto my path (**Psalm 119:105**). It is better to trust in the LORD than to put confidence in man (**Psalm 118:8**). There is a way which seemeth right unto a man, but the end thereof are the ways of death (**Proverbs 14:12**).*

If you were lead/led by a pencil, to draw you closer to Christ, will your picture come to life? Perhaps, it would be a still life.

Moreover, if you were drawn by a pencil from man's directions, which way are you being led/lead?

Furthermore, if we are supposed to look like Christ, then will your image come to life? If not, then perhaps, you would have the opportunity to erase your mistakes, and start over. But, if you were penned/pinned, would your writes/rights come to life, or will you be setup to be pinned/penned through a conned-track/contract, where you can't wrestle your way out? Perhaps, you can't get up, nor can you erase your errors.

Have you ever drawn yourself to a sign too quickly to stop? It can be impatience for reading the fine print, before signing your name. Maybe, you have a drive to get somewhere in life, but God's signs and wonders will keep you on track. If a train wheel is one inch off of the track, it cannot get on rail by itself. If you where a ruler away from God, then how can you stay connected to God if someone else is your ruler, who trains you, by their will/wheel, to keep you on their track? If man doesn't train in the ways of God, then isn't man's track record going in a different direction, other than God's training wills/wheels? We cannot get on track by ourselves, and man (by himself) will re-lure you in the opposite direction. That's why we all need the writes/rights of God to keep us on course.

> *All scripture is given by inspiration of God, and is profitable for doctrine, for reproof, for correction, for instruction in righteousness* **(2 Timothy 3:16)**:

To be re-lured in a wrong direction, may keep you miles away from your destination. But, if you choose God to be The Ruler of your life, then you may be only a foot from your dream. Isn't a ruler also a foot?

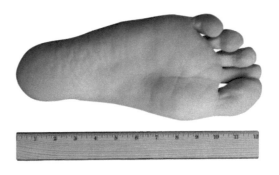

With that being said, then God isn't that far from you. As a ruler equals to a foot, then shouldn't your walk be in the ways of God, if He is your Ruler?

> *Lest Satan should get an advantage of us: for we are not ignorant of his devices* **(2 Corinthians 2:11)**. *If we live in the Spirit, let us also walk in the Spirit* **(Galatians 5:25)**.

A ruler created by man, is also assumed to be evenly measured to one foot, with all 12 inches measuring exactly the same. But, do you not know that no one in this world is perfect?

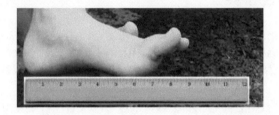

Many of our feet are shorter than a ruler made of man. But, we all come short of the glory of God, who is Ruler over us. We may try to reach perfection, but neither one of us are 100% correct. Therefore, why trust in man's judgment, when God, being our Ruler, goes beyond the measure of man?

> *Who can understand his errors? cleanse thou me from secret faults* ***(Psalm 19:12)***.

God also measures time, the weight of water, and He supplies to each one of us, a measure of faith, what a man's ruler has no authority over. If you don't have one foot to walk on, then God is still your Ruler to guide your walk of faith through Him. If your walk, in God, are feet away, then can't you see your journey ahead? Moreover, if your walk are blocks away from the Lord, then who's blocking your vision?

> *Where there is no vision, the people perish: but he that keepeth the law, happy is he* ***(Proverbs 29:18)***. *And shall say, Cast ye up, cast ye up, prepare the way, take up the stumblingblock out of the way of my people* ***(Isaiah 57:14)***.

Have you ever looked at a footage and asked yourself, "Can I be like that someday?" If God has ordained a purpose for each one of us, then what would be the length of your walk in footage, to reach another person's destiny? That one mile equals to 5,280 feet, and if your legs were worn out, how many steps will it take you to master, or more less, learn someone else's ordained gift, that isn't the call that God had for you?

"CAN YOUR FAITH GO THE EXTRA MILE TO WALK A FOOTAGE ON WATER? MOREOVER, HOW STRONG IS YOUR FAITH WALK ON FOOTAGE, SO OTHERS CAN SEE/SEA LIKE YOU?"

Picture this:

"CAN YOU STAND THE TEST OF THIS FOOTAGE ON WATER?"

A man's heart deviseth his way: but the LORD directeth his steps ***(Proverbs 16:9)***.

It's amazing how someone may get jealous of another person's talents. In time, they will stretch themselves, to put their foot in their mouth. Perhaps, they would get bent out of shape by a long stretch. But, why talk bad of someone that you wish to be like?

> *For who maketh thee to differ from another? and what hast thou that didst not receive? now if thou didst receive it, why dost thou glory, as if thou hadst not received it* **(1 Corinthians 4:7)**?

Moreover, if you have thoughts to endorse yourself into someone else's gifts, don't you know that God will bless you with talents beyond your wildest dreams? Many people are blessed with talents to put their foot in a home cooked meal.

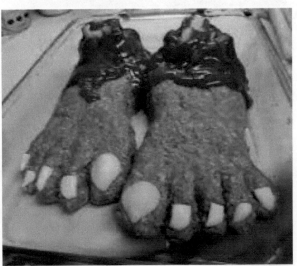

"STICKING YOUR TOES INTO A FINE MEAL"

Your blessings will come in perfect timing. No one can measure time like God. He measures time perfectly, as the Ruler that He is. That God is our Ruler, don't think of Him as a straight line to measure our distance. Think of God, our Ruler, as the answer to the straight narrow path that will keep us in line, as we go the distance, for eternal life, through His word.

> *And we know that all things work together for good to them that love God, to them who are the called according to his purpose **(Romans 8:28)**.*

"Does Your Toes Lead Your Souls"

That your toes are the front of your feet, do they guide your walk? Do the soles of your feet lead you in the walks of life, or is your walk led by your soul for Christ? Are you sold out for Christ, or is the bottom of your feet soled out, as an excuse not to walk in Christ?

*Blessed is the man that walketh not in the counsel of the ungodly, nor standeth in the way of sinners, nor sitteth in the seat of the scornful **(Psalm 1:1)**. As ye have therefore received Christ Jesus the Lord, so walk ye in him **(Colossians 2:6)**:*

I've heard the expression, "I sure did put my foot in my mouth this time!" The words that we speak will alter our walks of life, whether it's positive or negative. Isn't it funny, that when someone puts their foot in their mouth,

their mouth drops to the floor?

**"Results After Putting His Foot
In His Mouth"**

Perhaps, the mouth just traded places with the foot. Now, you really have to stand on the words that you speak. But, how can you stand to be on one foot without balance. Perhaps, you will need someone to lean on, because you put yourself in an awkward position to hop to conclusions.

> *Keep thy foot when thou goest to the house of God, and be more ready to hear, than to give the sacrifice of fools: for they consider not that they do evil. Be not rash with thy mouth, and let not thine heart be hasty to utter any thing before God: for God is in heaven, and thou upon earth: therefore let thy words be few. For a dream cometh through the multitude of business; and a fool's voice is known by multitude of words* **(Ecclesiastes 5:1-3)**.

It's amazing how the standards/standings of your feet are what the rest of your body depends on. Just because the feet are at bottom, and the head is at the top, doesn't make the feet the cause of being less important than the head. The bottom is as important as the top. If your head was formed first, and the feet were formed last, doesn't mean that they don't equal to the same portion. Isn't God the first and the last? He is also the same from beginning to end.

> *I am Alpha and Omega, the beginning and the end, the first and the last* **(Revelation 22:13)**.

Moreover, if the thinking of your mind is not of God, it will effect your walk. But, if your walk is not of Christ, just as your eyes may see, you will still be spiritually blind. Therefore, if your feet are not in your ordained path, then how can you face forward in your thoughts, if it is impossible to get ahead/a head?

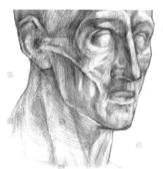

CAN'T GET AHEAD/A HEAD TO CONNECT WITH YOURSELF, THEN HOW WILL YOU LEAD OTHERS?

*In whom the god of this world hath blinded the minds of them which believe not, lest the light of the glorious gospel of Christ, who is the image of God, should shine unto them **(2 Corinthians 4:4)**. If we live in the Spirit, let us also walk in the Spirit **(Galatians 5:25)**. Ye shall walk in all the ways which the LORD your God hath commanded you, that ye may live, and that it may be well with you, and that ye may prolong your days in the land which ye shall possess **(Deuteronomy 5:33)**.*

Aren't your feet carrying all of your weight? That your body is the creation of God, doesn't that make you all business? Therefore, the foot of a corporation is as important as the head of the creation. You need both for your business to operate, as well as everything in between.

*But now are they many members, yet but one body. And the eye cannot say unto the hand, I have no need of thee: nor again the head to the feet, I have no need of you **(1 Corinthians 12:20-21)**.*

But, that we are God's creation, our business is His business. When He shows out for us, that makes us His show business.

**"GOD'S HOLY-WOOD SHOW BUSINESS
SHINING WITH THE STARS"**

If we are soled out/sold out, because of no base to lean on, then God will make a way out of no way. He just wants us to be soled out/sold out for Him.

> *Behold, I will do a new thing; now it shall spring forth; shall ye not know it? I will even make a way in the wilderness, and rivers in the desert* **(Isaiah 43:19)**.

"Why Place An 'X' For Christ"

It's amazing how many people will write, "Merry Xmas" instead of "Merry Christmas". Are you trying to shorthand Christ with an "X" in the place of His name?

If time is money, and it takes less of our/hour time to write an "X" versus writing/righting "Christ", then why worry about a few more seconds of our writes/rights, if the Lord is the creator of time? That the Lord created time, how can we make up for time better than the creator?

> *In the beginning God created the heaven and the earth. And the earth was without form, and void; and*

darkness was upon the face of the deep. And the Spirit of God moved upon the face of the waters. And God said, Let there be light: and there was light. And God saw the light, that it was good: and God divided the light from the darkness. And God called the light Day, and the darkness he called Night. And the evening and the morning were the first day **(Genesis 1:1-5)**.

That change is money, are you trying to shortchange Christ with an "X"? How would you feel if you were shortchanged with "X" amount of dollars, or "X" amount of change less than you were supposed to receive?

The days of his youth hast thou shortened: thou hast covered him with shame. Selah **(Psalm 89:45)**.

There are many times that the Lord has given us a huge change, and we don't recognize His riches working though us. Perhaps, many are trying to X Christ out all together. But, why would you X out the one who died for our sins, to save our lives? On the flipside, how can you save your own life by Xing Christ out of your life?

**"EVEN THOUGH JESUS WAS STONED,
HE IS STILL THE ROCK!"**

Furthermore, when Christ died for our sins, He cross multiplied for our lives, because He lives in us. Jesus is The Rock, and Earth is also a rock that Jesus was crucified on. But, isn't it amazing that Jesus is bigger than the earth? Jesus was stoned, and yet, He is still The Rock! When they stoned Christ, that just made Him the bigger Rock. That Jesus is The Rock, as He is as still/steel as He can be, then He stands firm to His word, as He is no one to medal/meddle with, because Jesus is more precious than gold. When we try to rock, like Jesus, we waiver back and forth, like a rocking chair. Therefore, how can we reach the level of Jesus' gold/goal, for our lives, without His help?

> There is therefore now no condemnation to them which
> are in Christ Jesus, who walk not after the flesh, but
> after the Spirit. For the law of the Spirit of life in Christ
> Jesus hath made me free from the law of sin and
> death. For what the law could not do, in that it was

*weak through the flesh, God sending his own Son in the likeness of sinful flesh, and for sin, condemned sin in the flesh: That the righteousness of the law might be fulfilled in us, who walk not after the flesh, but after the Spirit. For they that are after the flesh do mind the things of the flesh; but they that are after the Spirit the things of the Spirit **(Romans 8:1-5)**. For my thoughts are not your thoughts, neither are your ways my ways, saith the LORD. For as the heavens are higher than the earth, so are my ways higher than your ways, and my thoughts than your thoughts **(Isaiah 55:8-9)**.*

Instead of changing Christ to an "X", doesn't it make plenty of sense/cents to change with Christ? The X amount that we give Christ, there's a greater X amount of change that He profits us in return. I'd rather do a cross-examination for Christ, than to "X"/exit Him out of my life.

If you banked on man, who seems to always put you in the negative, because man isn't always truthful, then it makes sense/cents for change, to bank on Christ, who's always in the positive. Isn't it amazing, that if you are a true profit/prophet for Christ, you will get a bigger return in blessings?

*Wherein in time past ye walked according to the course of this world, according to the prince of the power of the air, the spirit that now worketh in the children of disobedience: Among whom also we all had our conversation in times past in the lusts of our flesh, fulfilling the desires of the flesh and of the mind; and were by nature the children of wrath, even as others **(Ephesians 2:2-3)**. For the LORD God is a sun and shield: the LORD will give grace and glory: no good thing will he withhold from them that walk uprightly **(Psalm 84:11)**.*

"A Hoary Story"

How valuable is your hair? It is said that knowledge is money. Therefore, isn't wisdom also a wealth of riches? If the hairs on your head are silver, then how rich are you in wisdom? Perhaps, the hair flow of silver treasures are flourishing from your gold-mind/goldmine.

Do you bank on the wisdom that God has given you? If so, then have you checked the account of your hairs? Isn't it amazing how God knows the count of each one of our hairs? God also knows our value more than we know ourselves.

> *Commit thy works unto the LORD, and thy thoughts shall be established **(Proverbs 16:3)**. But even the very hairs of your head are all numbered. Fear not therefore: ye are of more value than many sparrows **(Luke 12:7)**.*

If you, as a generation of silver, cannot keep up with the hair count from your heads, then why ask for millions of dollars that are well over the hairs that you refused to count? Now, if you could keep up with the count of your hairs, then you would have counted rolls of silver. Perhaps, you will be rolling in dough.

> *For wisdom is a defence, and money is a defence: but the excellency of knowledge is, that wisdom giveth life to them that have it **(Ecclesiastes 7:12)**.*

Furthermore, you will see dollar signs ($).

*With thy wisdom and with thine understanding thou
hast gotten thee riches, and hast gotten gold and silver
into thy treasures **(Ezekiel 28:4)**:*

If you lost some of your hairs of silver, do you know
how many hairs you have left? Furthermore, how
much have you lost in rolls? Have you been ripped
off? Perhaps, the count of hairs are too much for you
to handle! Then, how can one manage the amount in
which you are wishing for in millions of dollars?

*For which of you, intending to build a tower, sitteth not
down first, and counteth the cost, whether he have
sufficient to finish it? Lest haply, after he hath laid the
foundation, and is not able to finish it, all that behold it
begin to mock him, Saying, This man began to build,
and was not able to finish **(Luke 14:28-30)**.*

"In The Middle Of Something"

One day I was riding a bus, going into the city of Chicago. As I was sitting on one side, another passenger was seated across from me.

I asked him if he would be interested in purchasing a book. I also stated that I am the Author, and asked if he supports a positive cause. He didn't have a cell phone in his hand, papers, or anything. He was just looking around. But, he told me, "Right now, I'm in the middle of something!" I said, "Really sir? You know what? I'm in the middle of something too. I'm in the middle of this bus just like you are. But, when you step off of the bus, you'll still be in the middle of something, because the world is shaped like a sphere.

*Though I walk in the midst of trouble, thou wilt revive me: thou shalt stretch forth thine hand against the wrath of mine enemies, and thy right hand shall save me **(Psalm 138:7)**.*

Whatever point you stand in life, you're the center of God. I tell you what, if you take a bowling ball, which is the shape of Earth, wherever your finger points on that bowling ball, is where your finger stands. Perhaps, that's where we stand in life. When that bowling ball opens to a flat surface, where your finger points, will be the center point.

*Have ye not known? have ye not heard? hath it not been told you from the beginning? have ye not understood from the foundations of the earth? It is he that sitteth upon the circle of the earth, and the inhabitants thereof are as grasshoppers; that stretcheth out the heavens as a curtain, and spreadeth them out as a tent to dwell in **(Isaiah 40:21-22)**:*

When you go to bed, you may not be in the center of your bed like you're the center of God, but you will be somewhere in the middle.

When you go to sleep, you're still in the middle of something. You're in the middle of a dream." Then I replied, "Sir, that wasn't a very good excuse. We're always in the middle of something. You'll have to come better than that. When you roll off of your bed from the middle of a wild dream, number one, you will no longer be in the middle of that wild dream; number two, you won't be in the middle of your bed; number three, you will be somewhere in the middle of the floor. Moreover, Earth, in which we are in the center of is also in the hand of God.

> *In his hand are the deep places of the earth: the strength of the hills is his also **(Psalm 95:4)**.*

"Are Your Wishes Bottled Up?"

It has been said, "If it came in a bottle, everyone would have a great body."

Perhaps, if the things that we wish to accomplish were that simple, where a great body supplement were to come in a bottle, how much would the cost be for each bottle? In the place of bottles, which would arrive to a high expense, God has provided for us cans, without a cost, in all that we have a desire to achieve.

I can do all things through Christ which strengtheneth me (Philippians 4:13).

Just confess with your mouth that you can, and don't be bottled up with cannots.

> *And for me, that utterance may be given unto me, that I may open my mouth boldly, to make known the mystery of the gospel, For which I am an ambassador in bonds: that therein I may speak boldly, as I ought to speak* **(Ephesians 6:19-20)**.

If you wish to stay bottled in doubtful thinking, it will cost you a price that you will be unable to pay.

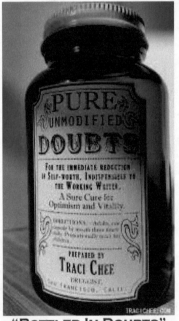

"BOTTLED IN DOUBTS"

> *And no man putteth new wine into old bottles: else the new wine doth burst the bottles, and the wine is spilled, and the bottles will be marred: but new wine must be put into new bottles* **(Mark 2:22)**.

Moreover, if the words of your mouth might get you tangled into cannots/can-knots, then how would you become loosened from bondage? If you speak doubts that will form into cannots/can-knots, then you will have strongholds tighter than strings attached.

"Can-Knot"

Stand fast therefore in the liberty wherewith Christ hath made us free, and be not entangled again with the yoke of bondage (Galatians 5:1).

If you have a difficult time getting a string unattached, then how much more complicated will it be to untangle a can-knot without getting wounded?

"Bottled Up In A Can Knot, but I can
see right through you"

I said, I will answer also my part, I also will shew mine opinion. For I am full of matter, the spirit within me constraineth me. Behold, my belly is as wine which hath no vent; it is ready to burst like new bottles. I will speak, that I may be refreshed: I will open my lips and answer (Job 32:17-20).

"Believing In Yourself"

Stay consistent, and not resistant.

If you leave, you can't receive.

If you don't stay on it, you'll postpone it, and you will give up on wanting it.

If you don't be bold, then you can't reach your goal.

If you are tender, then you will surrender.

If you don't stay in the game, you can't win to fame.

If you don't have a plan, then what foundation do you have to stand?

If you don't have a base, then how can you begin to win the race?

If you don't face your struggles, then how can you defeat your troubles?

If you aren't keen on your dreams, then how can you redeem your means?

If you don't retrieve what you believe, then how can you get back what you once lacked?

If you leave be a positive thought-ation, then how can you stay true to follow through to believe your imagination?

If you want to excel, to reach a higher scale, then be careful who you tell, if you want to prevail.

If you don't pray about, what negative say will come out of it, for you to doubt it?

If you believe in yourself, that in itself is a gain of wealth.

> *Every good gift and every perfect gift is from above, and cometh down from the Father of lights, with whom is no variableness, neither shadow of turning **(James 1:17)**. Have not I commanded thee? Be strong and of a good courage; be not afraid, neither be thou dismayed: for the LORD thy God is with thee whithersoever thou goest **(Joshua 1:9)**. But seek ye first the kingdom of God, and his righteousness; and all these things shall be added unto you **(Matthew 6:33)**. Wherefore seeing we also are compassed about with so great a cloud of witnesses, let us lay aside every weight, and the sin which doth so easily beset us, and let us run with patience the race that is set before us **(Hebrews 12:1)**, Commit thy works unto the LORD, and thy thoughts shall be established **(Proverbs 16:3)**. This book of the law shall not depart out of thy mouth; but thou shalt meditate therein day and night, that thou mayest observe to do according to all that is written therein: for then thou shalt make thy way prosperous, and then thou shalt have good success **(Joshua 1:8)**. And thou say in thine heart, My power and the might of mine hand hath gotten me this wealth. But thou shalt remember the LORD thy God: for it is he that giveth thee power to get wealth, that he may establish his covenant which he sware unto thy fathers, as it is this day **(Deuteronomy 8:17-18)**.*

"Proving That God Is Good Alpha-braically"

Coming from an Alpha-braic/algebraic perspective, to prove that GOD is GOOD:

In this Alpha-matical (mathematical) equation, the word "is" is equivalent to equal (=).

Example: 1 + 1 is 2. In the same manner, 1 + 1 = 2.

Therefore, knowing that GOD is GOOD, in the like manner, we arrive to:

GOD = GOOD.

The letter "O" is the abbreviation for "One". Therefore:

O = One = 1, and also

Alpha = First = 1st = 1

In this Alpha-matical/mathematical equation, wherever there is an "O", replace it with a "1":

GOD = GOOD

G(1)D = G(1)(1)D

1GD = 1^2GD

One (1) to any power is still one (1). That's why God is God all by Himself. Perhaps, that's because God is all power in Himself, and He is One!

Giving you:

$$1GD = 1GD$$

$$GD = GD$$

Therefore, GOD is GOOD! Moreover, GOD is GOD!

Since God is Alpha and Omega, I will prove that GOD is GOOD from an Omega's perspective:

$$O_1 = \text{Omega, and } O_2 = \text{One} = 1$$

$$G(O_1)D = G(O_1)(O_2)D$$

$$G(\text{Omega})D = G(\text{Omega})(1)D$$

$$\text{GOmegaD} = \text{GOmega(1)D}$$
GO mega! GO mega! ♪♪

DEFINITION OF MEGA — VERY LARGE; HUGE.

Whatever is multiplied by "1", it will equal to itself. Furthermore, I will combine all like letters together, giving me:

$$\text{GODmega} = (1)\text{GODmega}$$

$$\text{GODmega} = \text{GODmega}$$

Isn't GOD GOOD, and isn't GOD also OMEGA? He is GOD of all gods, and it reconfirms that He is GOD all by Himself, for the reason that He is 1. Now, you do the math!

> *Great is our Lord, and of great power: his understanding is infinite* **(Psalm 147:5)**. *And when he was gone forth into the way, there came one running, and kneeled to him, and asked him, Good Master, what shall I do that I may inherit eternal life? And Jesus said unto him, Why callest thou me good? there is none good but one, that is God* **(Mark 10:17-18)**. *I am Alpha and Omega, the beginning and the end, the first and the last* **(Revelation 22:13)**.

CHAPTER 2

"PLAY ON WORDS"

"In God's Presence/Presents"

To be in God's presence/presents is the best presence/presents that you can have. If you are in God's presence/presents, then you will be amazed with His gifts. For the present time that we live in, is a gift for every moment that we're alive.

> *Thou wilt shew me the path of life: in thy presence is fullness of joy; at thy right hand there are pleasures for evermore (Psalm 16:11).*

Is not a gift a present? If you rejoice more in God's presence/presents, then He will bless you with more gifts. If you aren't open in God's presence/presents, then your gifts won't unfold. The Lord loves to rap in His word, as a gift to us, for strength, wisdom, and protection. Therefore, shouldn't we be in the unwrapping business of God's word to share His presence/presents, as a gift, with others, so they can be just, like Him/just like Him?

> *For the wages of sin is death; but the gift of God is eternal life through Jesus Christ our Lord (Romans 6:23).*

That God's word is a gift to us, if we meditate in His presence/presents for an hour of time each day, the Lord will capitalize on hour/our wisdom, for hour/our knowledge, day by day. If knowledge is power, then wouldn't the word of God make you a profit/prophet in the presence/presents of time?

*Serve the LORD with gladness: come before his presence with singing **(Psalm 100:2)**.*

If we are a prophet/profit for God, then how much more will we receive in His riches, than if we were to prophet/profit for ourselves? If you don't receive in God's presence/presents, then would you appreciate His gifts? Moreover, if you don't give a gift, will you be presented a present?

> *Give, and it shall be given unto you; good measure, pressed down, shaken together, and running over, shall men give into your bosom. For with the same measure that ye mete withal it shall be measured to you again **(Luke 6:38)**.*

"A Free Will To Make Our Own Decisions"

The word says that we have a free will to make our own decisions. But, to make our own decisions will not make us free. It may come to a high expense.

And he said to them all, If any man will come after me, let him deny himself, and take up his cross daily, and follow me. For whosoever will save his life shall lose it: but whosoever will lose his life for my sake, the same shall save it (Luke 9:23-24).

It has also been said to write out the plan. But, just because we write out the plan, does not make it right. Moreover, it does not mean that our writes/rights will come to vision, nor does it mean that our plan would be in the making. We also have to speak what we want, and believe by faith.

*And the LORD answered me, and said Write the vision, and make it plain upon tables, that he may run that readeth it. For the vision is yet for an appointed time, but at the end it will surely come, it will not tarry **(Habakkuk 2:2-3)**. Jesus answered and said unto them, Verily I say unto you, if ye have faith, and doubt not, ye shall not only do this which is done to the fig tree, but also if ye shall say unto this mountain, Be thou removed, and be thou cast into the sea; it shall be done. And all things, whatsoever ye shall ask in prayer, believing, ye shall receive* **(Matthew 21:21-22)**.

God has given us the power over all things. Therefore, if God has given us a discernment, then we have the power to go overseas/over-sees (over what we see) by faith. Moreover, if we have power over a sea/see, then God's blessings reigns/rains over us, in an overflow.

*For God hath not given us the spirit of fear; but of power, and of love, and of a sound mind **(2 Timothy 1:7)**. Bring ye all the tithes into the storehouse, that there may be meat in mine house, and prove me now herewith, saith the LORD of hosts, if I will not open you the windows of heaven, and pour you out a blessing, that there shall not be room enough to receive it* **(Malachi 3:10)**.

Just because we have eyes to lookout, doesn't mean that we have the correct outlook on all situations. There are times that we overlook things in life, because we are not careful to look things over.

But, if we are careful, then we will look things over with full of care.

> *And why beholdest thou the mote that is in thy brother's eye, but considerest not the beam that is in thine own eye? Or how wilt thou say to thy brother, Let me pull out the mote out of thine eye; and, behold, a beam is in thine own eye? Thou hypocrite, first cast out the beam out of thine own eye; and then shalt thou see clearly to cast out the mote out of thy brother's eye* **(Matthew 7:3-5)**. *And the times of this ignorance God winked at; but now commandeth all men every where to repent* **(Acts 17:30)***:*

But, to be careful, we will also have to get our proper rest in God. If we get our rest, in the Lord, then He extends guidance to us for the rest of our lives by His will.

> *Rest in the LORD, and wait patiently for him: fret not thyself because of him who prospereth in his way, because of the man who bringeth wicked devices to pass* **(Psalm 37:7)**. *Howbeit when he, the Spirit of truth, is come, he will guide you into all truth: for he shall not speak of himself; but whatsoever he shall hear, that shall he speak: and he will shew you things to come* **(John 16:13)**.

135

"Catching A Blessing VS Catching A Bus"

If you stand in line to catch a bus, then why not stand in line for a blessing? A blessing will take you a lot farther than a bus. A bus will take you from city to city, but a blessing will take you to another state of mind. Moreover, a bus will take you no higher than a plain surface. Have you ever tried taking a bus overseas? How far do you think that you will get before you began to sink?

CAN YOU COUNT ON THIS BUS TO MAKE IT AS FAR AS PETER, OR DOES PETER GET BUSTED ON THE COUNT OF HIS DOUBT AND UNBELIEF? MOREOVER, HOW FAR, FROM 1 TO 1000, CAN YOU COUNT ON YOUR LIFE, BEFORE YOUR NUMBER COMES TO AN END?

But, a blessing will take you over a sea/see, because it will give you unexpected surprises that will work for your good. A blessing will also take you beyond a plane/plain surface. Therefore, it will take you over the air, for greater news that's out of this world.

A bus that takes you from city to city, they are places that you've experienced before. But, a blessing will take you places that are higher than you've ever thought to ask.

> *Now it shall come to pass, if you diligently obey the voice of the LORD your God, to observe carefully all His commandments which I command you today, that the LORD your God will set you high above all nations of the earth. And all these blessings shall come upon you and overtake you, because you obey the voice of the LORD your God: Blessed shall you be in the city, and blessed shall you be in the country **(Deuteronomy 28:1-3-NKJV)**.*

With a bus ride, you may have one return trip, but a blessing will take you on a journey for life, with many returns of profits.

> *Being confident of this very thing, that he which hath begun a work in you will perform it until the day of Jesus Christ **(Philippians 1:6)**: Commit thy works unto the LORD, and thy thoughts shall be established **(Proverbs 16:3)**. Fear thou not; for I am with thee: be not dismayed; for I am thy God: I will strengthen thee; yea, I will help thee; I will uphold thee with the right hand of my righteousness **(Isaiah 41:10)**.*

A bus is driven by a human who guides the wheel. They can also make mistakes along the way, and they can make you late for your appointment. But, when God has a divined blessing for our lives, His will is to give us drive, and guide us through our appointed times, so that we will not be late. God has a purpose for each of our lives, and He makes no mistakes. A car driven by man can be blown off track, but miracles driven by God will have you blown away, but you will still remain on track.

> *He is the Rock, his work is perfect: for all his ways are judgment: a God of truth and without iniquity, just and right is he **(Deuteronomy 32:4)**. There are many devices in a man's heart; nevertheless the counsel of the LORD, that shall stand **(Proverbs 19:21)**. Thou art the God that doest wonders: thou hast declared thy strength among the people **(Psalm 77:14)**. And Jesus looking upon them saith, With men it is impossible, but not with God: for with God all things are possible **(Mark 10:27)**.*

"Can You Tell Time?"

A friend came over to help me with a book project one afternoon. It was starting to get late, while we were both sitting at the kitchen table, working on the project.

She asked: Can I sit where you're sitting?

I responded: Why do you want to sit where I'm sitting? I don't think the chair can take but one person. If you can sit in the same seat where I'm sitting, without the chair falling apart, then I will get the feel of walking in your shoes.

She responded: Okay smarty, I want to exchange seats.

I stated: Ahhhhhhh (As if I didn't already know!) But, why do you want to exchange seats?

She: So I can keep an eye on the time.

Me: Uh, you don't trust me with the time?

She: No! You're good with numbers, and you're good with math, but you can't tell time.

Me: Ain't that about a trip! I can't tell time! You know what? I know that I can't tell time, because when I tell time to stop, it never listens, it keeps running. Time has three hands, but it has no ears. By the way, can you tell a baby?

Isn't that something, you can't tell a baby, and then complain that I can't tell time? You know, a baby has ears, and time doesn't. Furthermore, time is God's baby, so why do you need to keep an eye on what God already has full control over? Because God is in control of time, time is always good, because it is seasoned to God's taste. There's no wonder why things happen in perfect timing.

Time and a baby, they act just alike. You know why? Because, a baby was born in time.

"A Baby Is Born In The Womb Of Time"

That's why they act so much alike. Time has no legs, and they have no feet. That's why it runs with its hands. On the other hand, or shall I say, "...the second hand," a baby isn't so good with their legs or feet, because they were born in time, perhaps, by the second. But, they're so quick with their hands, just like time.

Time has three hands, and they do have one eye. Isn't that why it's called a watch? Can you tell time what to do or say in a sign language? Can you tell a baby what to do or say in a sign language, that was just born in time? Perhaps, their eyes are still closed, so what can they watch? Time is like a baby. You have to value it every moment you get. Furthermore, that peace comes in time, how many people can control peace? If not too many, then who has the power to tell time?

He hath made every thing beautiful in his time: also he hath set the world in their heart, so that no man can find out the work that God maketh from the beginning to the end **(Ecclesiastes 3:11)**. *But of that day and that hour knoweth no man, no, not the angels which are in heaven, neither the Son, but the Father. Take ye heed, watch and pray: for ye know not when the time is* **(Mark 13:32-33)**.

We all have a time window in life, because we were all born into a window of time.

"A TIME WINDOW"

Therefore, because you were born in the presence of your mothers' womb, and your mother was born in time, before you, then do you have the right to tell your mother? Then, what gives you the power to tell time, that was created way before your mother? Furthermore,
that your mother does not allow you to tell her, as she was born into a "Grand Old Time" of life, before you, then what makes you think that you can tell time, who is a Great Granny to you?

That time passes in a day, and as time also burns by the sun, a day vanishes at no return. Can you reinvent the wheel/will of the sun, day by day? Perhaps, you will be burned out, because the sun is a fireball of light. Can you roll like that? Moreover, if you made a mistake in the time of day, can you tell time to move backward? Can you rush time when it is having its moment of peace? It's amazing how we try to blow time, but does that speed it up?

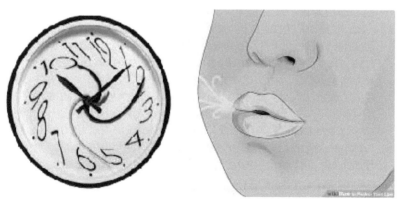

"BLOWING TIME THROUGH A RUSH HOUR"

If it is not so, then who has control over telling time how to operate, but God? In conclusion, that time is God's baby, then why should anyone have business telling a creation that only functions under God's control? "Time" is to enjoy, as we grow in life, but "Time" is not for us to teach a lesson, because we learn lessons through "Time".

*And the Lord said unto Joshua, Fear them not: for I have delivered them into thine hand; there shall not a man of them stand before thee. Joshua therefore came unto them suddenly, and went up from Gil'gal all night. And the LORD discomfited them before Israel, and slew them with a great slaughter at Gib'-e-on, and chased them along the way that goeth up to Beth-ho'-ron, and smote them to A-ze-kah, and unto Mak-ke'-dah. And it came to pass, as they fled from before Israel, and were in the going down to Beth-ho'-ron, that the LORD cast down great stones from heaven upon them unto A-ze'-kah, and they died: they were more which died with hailstones than they whom the children of Israel slew with the sword. Then spake Joshua to the LORD in the day when the LORD delivered up the Am'-or-ites before the children of Israel, and he said in the sight of Israel, Sun, stand thou still upon Gib'-e-on; and thou, Moon, in the valley of Aj'-a-lon. And the sun stood still, and the moon stayed, until the people had avenged themselves upon their enemies. Is not this written in the book of Ja'-sher? So the sun stood still in the midst of heaven, and hasted not to go down about a whole day **(Joshua 10:8-13)**. For whatsoever things were written aforetime were written for our learning, that we through patience and comfort of the scriptures might have hope **(Romans 15:4)**.*

"Unwholesome VS The Whole Sum"

If the words that you speak are unwholesome, then they will come back broken apart in sums of pieces, and they will not return whole. Perhaps, the whole sum of words that you speak can make you or break you.

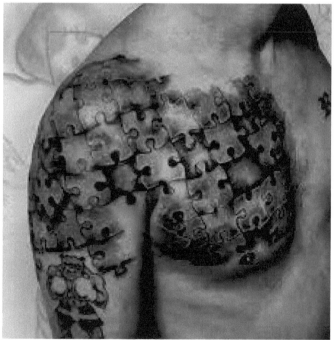

IF WE ARE BROKEN FOR BEING PUZZLED BY THE WORDS THAT WE SPEAK, THEN WE NEED TO PIECE OURSELVES TOGETHER, FOR A BETTER PEACE OF MIND.

Let no corrupt communication proceed out of your mouth, but that which is good to the use of edifying,

that it may minister grace unto the hearers
*(**Ephesians 4:29**). Death and life are in the power of*
the tongue: and they that love it shall eat the fruit
*thereof (**Proverbs 18:21**).*

If a puzzle is being put together, and some of the
pieces are not in the image, then how can you see the
clear vision of the whole picture? If the whole truth is
not revealed, then what part of the puzzle is missing?

**IF THE HEART OF THE PUZZLE IS MISSING, THEN IS THE SOUL
OF THE IMAGE STOLEN?**

From whom the whole body fitly joined together and
compacted by that which every joint supplieth,
according to the effectual working in the measure of
every part, maketh increase of the body unto the
*edifying of itself in love (**Ephesians 4:16**).*

If you had a prison term, for not telling the whole
story, and your prison time was putting the puzzle
together, on how you got there, how long will it take

you to figure out the solution to your problem that's 5,000 pieces to the puzzle?

Therefore, tell the whole truth, in the summation of a single image, versus 5,000 pieces, where sums/some of the pieces to the story may easily be lost. Perhaps, you would feel better, in having something to cheese about, because the image will not come back void. It will be a single craft image. That's connecting all of the pieces together in one visual, as it aligns with truth.

> For as the body is one, and hath many members, and all the members of that one body, being many, are one body: so also is Christ. For by one Spirit are we all baptized into one body, whether we be Jews or Gentiles, whether we be bond or free; and have been all made to drink into one Spirit. For the body is not one member, but many. If the foot shall say, because I am not the hand , I am not of the body; is it therefore

*not of the body? And if the ear shall say, Because I am not the eye, I am not of the body; is it therefore not of the body? If the whole body were an eye, where were the hearing? If the whole were hearing, where were the smelling? But now hath God set the members every one of them in the body, as it hath pleased him. And if they were all one member, where were the body? But now are they many members, yet but one body. And the eye cannot say unto the hand, I have no need of thee: nor again the head to the feet, I have no need of you. Nay, much more those members of the body, which seem to be more feeble, are necessary: And those members of the body, which we think to be less honourable, upon these we bestow more abundant honour; and our uncomely parts have more abundant comeliness. For our comely parts have no need: but God hath tempered the body together, having given more abundant honour to that part which lacked: That there should be no schism in the body; but that the members should have the same care one to another. And whether one member suffer, all the members suffer with it; or one member be honoured, all the members rejoice with it. Now ye are the body of Christ, and members in particular (**1 Corinthians 12:12-27**).*

It's amazing how a letter can be left out of a word, and change the whole meaning of that word.

Example: A storyline can be told to 10 people (one person at a time). By the time the storyline gets around to the 10th person, the storyline have been changed to something different. Perhaps, the storyline was turned into a story-lie. The individual that gave the message last, left the letter "n" out of line. Perhaps, the "n"/end of the storyline was left out from man's true word that was spoken.

FROM A STORYLINE TO A STORYLIE

But there were false prophets also among the people, even as there shall be false teachers among you, who privily shall bring in damnable heresies, even denying the Lord that bought them, and bring upon themselves swift destruction. And many shall follow their pernicious ways; by reason of whom the way of truth shall be evil spoken of **(2 Peter 2:1-2)**.

On the other hand, a word can be left out of a letter, and it will change the whole meaning of that letter.

Example: You have the qualifications for a particular career, and your resume is on point. But, your cover letter is missing one key word that will cause you to lose the opportunity.

As also in all his epistles, speaking in them of these things; in which are some things hared to be understood, which they that are unlearned and unstable wrest, as they do also the other scriptures, unto their own destruction. Ye therefore, beloved, seeing ye know these things before, beware lest ye also, being led away with the error of the wicked, fall from your own stedfastness. But grow in grace, and in the knowledge of our Lord and Saviour Jesus Christ. To him be glory both now and for ever. Amen' **(2 Peter 3:16-18)**.

That we all have a timeline for life, will your time lie on Satan's hands, or will you stay in line for God? If your time lies on Satan's hands, as he has lied on you before, he will re-lie/rely on you again, only to destroy your life. It's amazing how a word can change your life. But, on that note, even a letter. Satan comes to steal the letter "f" out of your life, to make it a lie. But, if you put your trust in the Lord, your Life line will be restored. Moreover, do you trust in a lifeline, that's spoken by man, to save your life, or do you put your trust in our savior Jesus Christ?

> *My times are in thy hand: deliver me from the hand of mine enemies, and from them that persecute me* **(Psalm 31:15)**. *Be sober, be vigilant; because your adversary the devil, as a roaring lion, walketh about, seeking whom he may devour* **(1 Peter 5:8)**: *The thief cometh not, but for to steal, and to kill, and to destroy: I am come that they might have life, and that they might have it more abundantly* **(John 10:10)**. *It is better to trust in the Lord than to put confidence in man* **(Psalm 118:8)**.

"Seeing From God's Point Of View And Not Your Point Of You"

Do you see from God's point of view, or do you only see from your point of you? That God is "I Am" and you present yourself as "I" (first person singular), then can you see I/eye to I/eye with God? If you see the way that God sees, or you look the way that God looks, then aren't you in the image as God? If you are in the same image as God, then how can you see from a different perspective than God?

> *So God created man in his own image, in the image of God created he him, male and female created he them* **(Genesis 1:27)**. *But the LORD said unto Samuel, Look not on his countenance, or on the height of his stature; because I have refused him: for man looketh on the outward appearance, but the LORD looketh on the heart* **(1 Samuel 16:7)**. *Woe unto them that are wise in their own eyes, and prudent in their own sight* **(Isaiah 5:21)***!*

God and Jesus come together as one, and they abide in us. Therefore, we have the power to do all things by them. If Jesus can walk over a sea/see, then why do your eyes take away your faith to sea/see beyond what it looks like?

"PETER AFRAID IN THE MIDDLE OF A SEA/SEE"

*And in the fourth watch of the night Jesus went unto them, walking on the sea. And when the disciples saw him walking on the sea, they were troubled, saying, It is a spirit; and they cried out for fear. But straightway Jesus spake unto them, saying, Be of good cheer; it is I; be not afraid. And Peter answered him and said, Lord, if it be thou, bid me come unto thee on the water. And he said, Come. And when Peter was come down out of the ship, he walked on the water, to go to Jesus. But when he saw the wind boisterous, he was afraid; and beginning to sink, he cried, saying, Lord, save me. And immediately Jesus stretched forth his hand, and caught him, and said unto him, O thou of little faith, wherefore didst thou doubt **(Matthew 14:25-31)**?*

Is it that we can look in the image that Jesus looks, but we can't sea/see how He seas/sees? Perhaps, Jesus can cease/see the water to be still. As most people, if not all, are afraid to lose their lives. Isn't it awful how many individuals may boldly dive into a debate that is not their fight, and will cause them their lives? But, we are so fearful of diving into water that will produce life. When you put your trust in the Lord, you can flow like Jordan, as a river of living waters. When you put your trust in God, He God's/guides/got your back, and you can make a slam dunk every time. Therefore, you can be on "Air" in the midst of a lot of fans, to deliver great news, on the story level of your dreams, while being given your best shot in life.

"FLOWING AS THE RIVERS OF JORDAN IN FRONT OF MANY FANS FOR THE AIR OF JORDAN'S"

That God is "I" (Roman Numeral One), and you present yourself as "I" (First Person Singular), where "I" = 1ˢᵗ(First) = 1(One), then are you One-on-One with God?

If so, then have you done your cross examination? Have you passed? If not, then how can you prove to be like Christ, who is also 1(One), with God?

> But to us there is but one God, the Father, of whom are all things, and we in him; and one Lord Jesus Christ, by whom are all things, and we by him *(**1 Corinthians 8:6**)*. For as the body is one, and hath many members, and all the members of that one body, being many, are one body: so also is Christ *(**1 Corinthians 12:12**)*. For even hereunto were ye called: because Christ also suffered for us, leaving us an example, that ye should follow his steps *(**1 Peter 2:21**)*: Be ye therefore perfect, even as your Father which is in heaven is perfect *(**Matthew 5:48**)*.

That there is a north side, south side, east side, and a west side, and each side tells a different story, then whose side are you on, or who will you side with? Furthermore, whose report do you believe? Are you on the same page with God? If not, then what's your story? Since God's thoughts are higher than our thoughts, then isn't the story that we live on lower than the story of God's? If the Lord lives on the top story of the highest building that ever exists, then why not trust in Him to build you up to the story level of His word?

> *And they said, Go to, let us build us a city and a tower, whose top may reach unto heaven; and let us make us a name, lest we be scattered abroad upon the face of the whole earth* **(Genesis 11:4)**.

We often speak the term, "The sky's the limit. If we know that there's a higher place than the sky, then why not choose plans for our lives that are higher than we can see? Why do we only settle for things that we can see, when our eyes may play tricks on us?

> *I will lift up mine eyes unto the hills, from whence cometh my help. My help cometh from the LORD, which made heaven and earth* **(Psalms 121:1-2)**. *For my thoughts are not your thoughts, neither are your ways my ways, saith the LORD. For as the heavens are higher than the earth, so are my ways higher than your ways, and my thoughts than your thoughts* **(Isaiah 55:8-9)**.

If you claim to be in your own world, then aren't you, also, in your own nation? If that is the case, then what's in your found-nation/foundation? Moreover, what's in your imagination, and in whose nation do you imagine to be your god?

> *According to the grace of God which is given unto me, as a wise masterbuilder, I have laid the foundation, and another buildeth thereon. But let every man take heed how he buildeth thereupon. For other foundation can no man lay than that is laid, which is Jesus Christ* **(1 Corinthians 3:10-11)**. *For thou shalt worship no other god: for the LORD, whose name is Jealous, is a jealous God* **(Exodus 34:14)**: *Thou shalt have no other gods before me* **(Exodus 20:3)**.

"Do You Bet Against Alpha?"

It's funny how many people try to tell the word, instead of speaking what the word tells us. On the other hand, aren't many people trying to tell the word what to say, in lieu of listening to what the word is revealing to us? Why do we, in many instances, try to turn a verse around to mean something else?

> *For false Christs and false prophets shall rise, and shall shew signs and wonders, to seduce, if it were possible, even the elect (**Mark 13:22**).*

If "u" were turned around, will not "u" come to an "n"? There are times that we put negative words into our own mouths. If you do that to yourself, would "you" come to "not" for good, or "not" for bad? God created you for a good purpose, so why turn yourself to not, from the way God created you?

you turned around is noʌ

> *Surely your turning of things upside down shall be esteemed as the potter's clay: for shall the work say of him that made it, He made it not? or shall the thing framed say of him that framed it, He had no understanding (**Isaiah 29:16**)?*

Remember the cereal with alphabets? If words are powerful to the point in which they can cause damage or destruction, then are there not serial/cereal killers?

> *How is the faithful city become an harlot! it was full of judgment; righteousness lodged in it; but now murderers **(Isaiah 1:21)**. Thy tongue deviseth mischiefs; like a sharp rasor, working deceitfully **(Psalm 52:2)**.*

If we are what we eat, then how are the letters that we swallow being formed in our system? Do the letters that we swallow have us cursed? Perhaps, we are puzzled by the words that we digest, that will make us unjust.

"A BIT OF WORD PLAY"

Furthermore, if every word that proceeds out of our mouths are formed with alphabets, and God is Alpha over all of us, then why are letters formed to bet against Alpha?

Alpha-bet

Moreover, in speaking about the cereal, "Alpha-Bits", that we eat our own words, do you trust in a "Bitcoin" over Alpha's Word?

If God doesn't lead us in the teachings of His word, will we not speak vice-versa instead of speaking by God's advice, through His every verse, that is written? Whose advice are we following, or whose vice are we adding? If we follow Christ, we won't fall low of Him.

> *For I testify unto every man that heareth the words of the prophecy of this book, If any man shall add unto these things, God shall add unto him the plagues that are written in this book: And if any man shall take away from the words of the book of this prophecy, God shall take away his part out of the book of life, and out of the holy city, and from the things which are written in this book* ***(Revelation 22:18-19)***.

If we bank on alphabets over God's word, then whom do we put our trust? Moreover, if we don't bank on God's word, and His word is life, then what will we profit from a trust that doesn't exist? Alphabets may spell positive words, but they also spell "Doubt" which is a negative. On that note, if God's word is all truth, then why bet against Alpha?

*Every word of God is pure: he is a shield unto them that put their trust in him. Add thou not unto his words, lest he reprove thee, and thou be found a liar **(Proverbs 30:5-6)**.*

"See VS Look"

How close are the words "see" and "look" in meaning? If you are seeing something, aren't you also looking at it? Furthermore, If the word "see" is looking in the mirror, isn't it looking at itself at "ees" (ease)?

SEE|ƎƎƨ

Now, if you see the word "look" in the mirror, wouldn't you see "kool" (cool)?

LOOK|ꓘOOꓶ

Well, aren't you kool (cool) if you are at ees (ease) with yourself?

> But the LORD said unto Samuel, Look not on his countenance, or on the height of his stature; because I have refused him: for the LORD seeth not as man seeth; for man looketh on the outward appearance, but the LORD looketh on the heart **(1 Samuel 16:7)**.

Let's paraphrase this aspect from another perspective. If a woman designs her eyes to look beautiful in a bad neighborhood, does that really mean that she can see beauty going down that same path of life? In addition, just because a person cannot see the part in a movie, does not mean that he or she can't look the part in the movie. If a person lost his or her vision, means that they can't see. Therefore, they can't look. But, if someone looks for light, doesn't mean that a person sees for light. To look for light is to search for light, but to see for light, is where the light is the evidence of how we see.

> *While we look not at the things which are seen, but at the things which are not seen: for the things which are seen are temporal; but the things which are not seen are eternal* **(2 Corinthians 4:18)**. *And there shall be no more curse: but the throne of God and of the Lamb shall be in it; and his servants shall serve him: And they shall see his face; and his name shall be in their foreheads. And there shall be no night there; and they need no candle, neither light of the sun; for the Lord God giveth them light: and they shall reign for ever and ever* **(Revelation 22:3-5)**.

In addition, just because he or she can't see beautiful, does not mean that he or she can't look beautiful.

Moreover, just because a person without vision cannot see with ees (ease), does not mean that he or she cannot look kool (cool).

*He hath made every thing beautiful in his time: also he hath set the world in their heart, so that no man can find out the work that God maketh from the beginning to the end **(Ecclesiastes 3:11)**. What man is he that feareth the LORD? him shall he teach in the way that he shall choose. His soul shall dwell at ease; and his seed shall inherit the earth **(Psalms 25:12-13)**.*

"A Water's Reflection
vs
A Mirror's Reflection"

The Lord has given us all LIFE, and for all, He has forgiven. When you are baptized under water, aren't you being cleansed, and isn't your LIFE being turned around for rite through Christ?

It is said that facts will reflect truth. That water is pure, doesn't it reveal truth? Moreover, isn't "LIFE" also turned around for rite, through the image of water?

*And this is the record, that God hath given to us eternal life, and this life is in his Son **(1 John 5:11)**.*

God made LigH+. How is LigH+ defined from a water's perspective?

It is obvious that "LIGHT" is also "RIGHT". Furthermore, Jesus is the Light. Didn't God create His Son, who is "Light" of the world? Aren't you blessed that Jesus came a cross (+), in your path, to save your life? Isn't that a plus (+)?

> *And God said, Let there be light: and there was light. And God saw the light, that it was good: and God divided the light from the darkness **(Genesis 1:3-4)**. Then spake Jesus again unto them, saying, I am the light of the world: he that followeth me shall not walk in darkness, but shall have the light of life* ***(John 8:12)***.

It's amazing how a right angle (in mathematics) can face in either direction, and still be right:

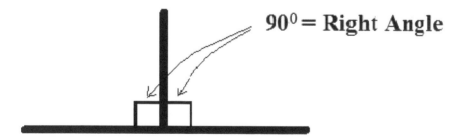

$90^0 =$ **Right Angle**

But, when the right angles are collaborated with itself, under water, doesn't it reveal a cross?

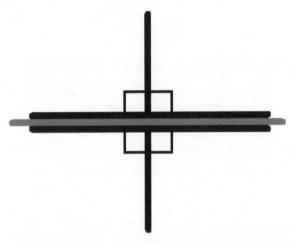

Study to shew thyself approved unto God, a workman that needeth not to be ashamed, rightly dividing the word of truth (2 Timothy 2:15).

Perhaps, that's why all angles are right, so that no one gets left behind. Moreover, didn't Jesus give us His all? Since that is the case, as every court has one, then what judgment is wrong about it?

For ways in which people are treated wrong feels unacceptable. But, the things that are correct, through Christ, are made collectables. In the sight of water, isn't "COLLEC+" also "COrrEC+"?

Since everything that is made by God is right, aren't we supposed to receive what He gives us, as a collectable, and then share with others? Moreover, when you feel that you have done everything correct, for a wrong doing, would you want to be judged by a correctional officer, by being given a space for life, in prison, and collect your thoughts, or would you rather be in the prison of the Lord, who offers you space for correction?

> *My son, despise not the chastening of the LORD; neither be weary of his correction: For whom the LORD loveth he correcteth; even as a father the son in whom he delighteth* **(Proverbs 3:11-12)**.

We should always put God first and foremost. As a roman numeral, God is "I" (Roman Numeral One).

Coming from a water's perspective, does God change His appearance?

But thou art the same, and thy years shall have no end
(Psalm 102:27).

Aren't we supposed to be in the image of God? When we characterize ourselves as a first person singular, we are also in the image of "I" (The Letter). Don't we appear as the image of God, who is "I" (Roman Numeral One)? But, our actions are different.

Now, if you take "I" (the letter), and multiply it 3 times, the summation will arrive to:

$$I \times I \times I = I^3 \text{ (I to the 3}^{rd}\text{ power)}$$

Therefore, a group of 1000 "I's" (people coming together) is:

$$I^{1000} \text{ (I to the one thousandth power)}$$

What about a nation of "I's"/eyes?

> *For as we have many members in one body, and all members have not the same office: So we, being many, are one body in Christ, and every one members one of another **(Romans 12:4-5)**.*

Look at Jesus, like Father, like Son:

$$\text{Father} \longleftarrow \textbf{II} \longrightarrow \text{Son}$$

(Roman Numeral 2)

> *But to us there is but one God, the Father, of whom are all things, and we in him; and one Lord Jesus Christ, by whom are all things, and we by him **(1 Corinthians 8:6)**. I and my Father are one **(John 10:30)**.*

God is One, and Jesus is One. They are two (2) I's/eyes looking upon us. Does a water's image change their appearance?

Jesus Christ the same yesterday, and to day, and for ever
(Hebrews 13:8).

Going a step further, the Father, Son, and Holy Ghost are three.

(Roman Numeral 3)

In the see/sea of water, as a roman numeral, aren't they the same?

For there are three that bear record in heaven, the Father, the Word, and the Holy Ghost: and these three are one. And there are three that bear witness in

earth, the Spirit, and the water, and the blood: and these three agree in one (1 John 5:7-8).

Picking up where I left off, with the nation of "I's", this time, I will use "I" (roman numeral one), by multiplying "I" 3 times:

$$I \times I \times I = I^3 = I$$

In the same likeness:

$$1 \times 1 \times 1 = 1^3 = 1$$

The points between them are to multiply our blessings, as they (the Father, Son, and Holy Ghost) come together as one. Isn't it amazing how mathematics doesn't have the power source to change the Father, Son, and Holy Ghost? Perhaps, it's because "They" are the highest power in one. They are also over all nations. But, if anyone of us were in the mix with the Father, the Son, and the Holy Ghost, as a roman numeral, we are presented as:

IV

(Roman Numeral 4)

Isn't something out of line? There seems to be conflict with two coming together. Aren't we bumping feet, and tripping on the Lord? We seem to be in disagreement. Perhaps, we are roman/roaming around, creating our own paths. What happened to the straight path that we are supposed to walk in? Look at roman numeral four (IV) under water:

It shows that we are bumping heads with the Lord. Perhaps, that's the reason that a person can start tripping, and bump heads at the same time. That God created the waters, as He created a sea/see, how do you sea/see yourself in the image of water?

> And God saw that the wickedness of man was great in the earth, and that every imagination of the thoughts of his heart was only evil continually. And it repented the LORD that he had made man on the earth, and it grieved him at his heart. And the LORD said, I will destroy man whom I have created from the face of the earth; both man, and beast, and the creeping thing, and the fowls of the air; for it repenteth me that I have made them *(Genesis 6:5-7)*.

Aren't we upside down?

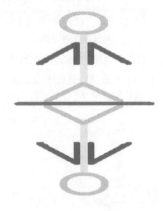

Again, doesn't water reveal truth? As man is poor/poured without the wisdom of God, we are as a glass turned upside down leaking tears of sadness. Therefore, without the guidance of the Lord, our knowledge is as an empty glass.

> Behold, the LORD maketh the earth empty, and maketh it waste, and turneth it upside down, and scattereth abroad the inhabitants thereof. The land shall be utterly emptied, and utterly spoiled: for the LORD hath spoken this word. The earth mourneth and fadeth away, the world languisheth and fadeth away, the haughty people of the earth do languish. The earth also is defiled under the inhabitants thereof; because they have transgressed the laws, changed the ordinance, broken the everlasting covenant **(Isaiah 24:1, and 3-5)**. Surely your turning of things upside down shall be esteemed as the potter's clay: for shall the work say of him that made it, He made me not? or shall the thing framed say of him that framed it, He had no understanding **(Isaiah 29:16)**?

But, by the counsel of God, we can be turned right side up and stay filled through the richness of His word, as He pours into us, joy and blessings. Isn't it amazing how the Lord uses reverse sea-chology (reverse psychology) to reveal truth? No matter what number of I's (the letter) that we power up to, as a nation, our power will never reach the highest margin of the Lord.

> *And it shall come to pass afterward, that I will pour out my spirit upon all flesh; and your sons and your daughters shall prophesy, your old men shall dream dreams, your young men shall see visions: And also upon the servants and upon the handmaids in those days will I pour out my spirit* **(Joel 2:28-29)**.

If "WE" work together, as a team, then "WE" can stand on top of water. But, if "WE" were under water, the reflection of water would reveal "WE" as a "ME".

"ME" would drown by myself. "ME" would also waiver, as the waves of the water. Water speaks truth, because it's clear. You see, "WE" has 2 letters, and 2 or more makes a team. "ME" also has 2 letters, but that's "ME" hanging in there by ME-self. Now, does that make "ME" true to myself? Actually, "ME"

hanging underwater by myself and surviving without a team, something's fishy about that.

Perhaps, "ME" by myself, underwater, will be well deserted/deserved. Therefore, "ME" would be a great dessert to the Well family of sharks and crocodiles. Underwater, without a team, "ME" would be well eaten alive.

"A DESSERT THAT IS 'WELL' APPRECIATED, AND SPEAKS VOLUMES TO THE SHARKS AND CROCODILES"

If you are good, wouldn't you be seen as good in the scene of water?

Moreover, if God was in a sea/see of water, does God change?

*For I am the LORD, I change not; therefore ye sons of Jacob are not consumed **(Malachi 3:6)**.*

Let's look at our "LIFE" from a mirror's perspective:

L I F E | Ǝ ꟻ I ⅃

Do you see life as an "E-file"? But, man made the mirror. Therefore, looking from a man's perspective, "LIFE" does not seem to be rite/right. If an e-file is bad instead of showing life, then how are you revealed from a mirror's perspective, if you were bad?

b A d | b A d

*The fool hath said in his heart, There is no God. They are corrupt, they have done abominable works, there is none that doeth good **(Psalm 14:1)**. There is a way which seemeth right unto a man, but the end thereof are the ways of death **(Proverbs 14:12)**. Every way of a man is right in his own eyes: but the LORD pondereth the hearts **(Proverbs 21:2)**.*

It looks like, coming from man's perspective, you will do bAd for bAd. God's will is not for us to turn bAd around for bAd. If you do not change the bAd, bAd will only repeat itself, until you change for the better.

> *And be not conformed to this world: but be ye transformed by the renewing of your mind, that ye may prove what is that good, and acceptable, and perfect, will of God (**Romans 12:2**). Woe unto them that seek deep to hide their counsel from the LORD, and their works are in the dark, and they say, Who seeth us? and who knoweth us (**Isaiah 29:15**)?*

Speaking about "bAd", if the devil looked himself in the mirror, how would he see himself?

devil liveb

IT LOOKS LIKE THE DEVIL WILL LIVE BACKWARDS BASED ON THE WORD OF GOD, AS THE "B" (IN THE MIRROR) STANDS FOR "BACKWARD". ALSO, DOING-EVIL (DEVIL) IS LIVING BACKWARDS.

> *A prudent man foreseeth the evil, and hideth himself: but the simple pass on, and are punished (**Proverbs 22:3**).*

Isn't it something how everything that is emitted in time has a spell on it? The things that we do, say, and think are manifested in our lives. Therefore, we have to be careful what we emit, because it turns back in time.

emit spelled backward is time.

Likewise, coming from a mirror's perspective, "emit" on the other side of the cell is doing "time":

emit|time

But all things that are reproved are made manifest by the light: for whatsoever doth make manifest is light **(Ephesians 5:13)**.

But, if we want to turn things around in time, for our lives, we have to emit the good, and not the bad. Furthermore, God just want a mite portion of our time, so that He can work mightily for us. Our time for God, should have no limit. Therefore, there shall be no time line for God.

limit spelled backward is timil.

$$tim \times (i) \times (l) =$$
$$tim\ (li) =$$
$$tim\ line = time\ line$$

Therefore, coming from a mirror's perspective, a "limit" faces a "time line":

limit|timil

If you look at the Father, Son, and Holy Ghost (as a roman numeral 3), from a mirror's perspective, will they change?

III | III

But, if we look at ourselves to be added in with the Father, Son, and Holy Ghost, as a roman numeral, don't we turn things around?

IV | VI

For none of us liveth to himself, and no man dieth to himself. For whether we live, we live unto the Lord; and whether we die, we die unto the Lord: whether we live therefore, or die, we are the Lord's ***(Romans 14:7-8)***.

Roman numeral 4 (IV) is revealed in a mirror's image as a roman numeral 6 (VI). As we are all associated as man in the bible, doesn't the number six (6) stand for man? Moreover, if "MAN" stands in the mirror, will he not see himself for who he is by name?

MAN | ИAM

Neither is there salvation in any other: for there is none other name under heaven given among men, whereby we must be saved ***(Acts 4:12)***. *A good* *name is rather to be chosen than great riches, and loving favour rather than silver and gold* **(Proverbs 22:1)**.

Everything in life has a purpose. In all things that we do, God already knew it was going to happen, and everything that exist has a name on it. Therefore, every name is spelled with its own unique purpose.

In whom also we have obtained an inheritance, being predestinated according to the purpose of him who worketh all things after the counsel of his own will: That we should be to the praise of his glory, who first trusted in Christ **(Ephesians 1:11-12)**.

If a roman numeral 4 (IV) was connected to itself, from a water's perspective, it would be seen as a roman numeral 9 (IX):

That the number 9 stands for divine completion, finality, and judgment, it looks like we would give ourselves complete attention. Therefore, if we, as a IV (roman numeral 4), tried to manipulate the spirit of the Father, Son, and Holy Ghost, a water's perspective will show each one of us coming to a dead-end, or to a final point in life.

He that believeth on me, as the scripture hath said, out of his belly shall flow rivers of living water **(John 7:38)**. *(But this spake he of the Spirit, which they that believe on him should receive: for the Holy Ghost was not yet given; because that Jesus was not yet glorified*

(John 7:39).) *But whosoever drinketh of the water that I shall give him shall never thirst; but the water that I shall give him shall be in him a well of water springing up into everlasting life (John 4:14).*

Also, as was stated earlier, if a roman numeral 4 (IV) looked itself in the mirror, it would see itself as man (roman numeral 6 = VI).

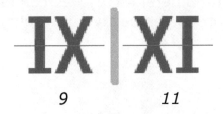

But, as the water and mirror perspectives collaborate, the roman numeral 4 (IV) is scened as a roman numeral 9 (IX), and a roman numeral 11 (XI):

IX | XI

9   11

That sure/shore looks like an emergency call, observing the whole picture of ourselves, or observing ourselves as a whole number. God is the Doctor of all doctors. If we are under His care, doesn't that make each one of us His emergency?

But it shall come to pass, if thou wilt not hearken unto the voice of the LORD thy God, to observe to do all his commandments and his statutes which I command thee this day; that all these curses shall come upon thee, and overtake thee: Cursed shalt thou be in the city, and cursed shalt thou be in the field. Cursed shall be thy basket and thy store. Cursed shall be the fruit of thy body, and the fruit of thy land, the increase of thy kine, and the flocks of thy sheep. Cursed shalt thou be when thou comest in, and cursed shalt thou be when thou goest out (Deuteronomy 28:15-19).

Both of the numbers, 9 and 11 stands for judgment. Perhaps, that's why we have to look at ourselves, before judging someone else. Moreover, would you rather be puzzled with this world, or jointed to God's puzzle, and stay connected?

> *And I saw the dead, small and great, stand before God; and the books were opened: and another book was opened, which is the book of life: and the dead were judged out of those things which were written in the books, according to their works. And the sea gave up the dead which were in it; and death and hell delivered up the dead which were in them: and they were judged every man according to their works. And death and hell were cast into the lake of fire. This is the second death. And whosoever was not found written in the book of life was cast into the lake of fire* **(Revelation 20:12-15)**.

When we stay connected with God, it is by prayer and His grace upon us. The number 5 stands for grace. If this number is shown as a roman numeral, it would be presented as "V". When two people come together for prayer in Jesus' name, and the prayer in which they are praying is in God's will, God will have grace upon them.

Grace

CAN YOU READ BETWEEN THE LINES?

*Wherefore we receiving a kingdom which cannot be moved, let us have grace, whereby we may serve God acceptably with reverence and godly fear: For our God is a consuming fire (**Hebrews 12:28-29**). As ye have therefore received Christ Jesus the Lord, so walk ye in him: Rooted and built up in him, and stablished in the faith, as ye have been taught, abounding therein with thanksgiving (**Colossians 2:6-7**).*

If you put your hand to a mirror, as 5 stands for grace, what collaboration does a mirror's image present when you put your hand to a test of glass?

Doesn't your hand and the reflection of your hand come together for grace and prayer? Perhaps, when we have grace through God, He deserves a high-five.

*Praying always with all prayer and supplication in the Spirit, and watching thereunto with all perseverance and supplication for all saints (**Ephesians 6:18**);*

Let's do a mirror and water collaboration demonstration:

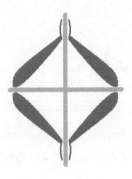

Doesn't it come together as a diamond? I call this my collaboration diamond-stration, instead of demonstration. It removes the demon from the source, through grace. A diamond is a precious gem. Isn't prayer and grace also a precious exercise for our everyday workout? It will make you stronger, sharper, brighter, and give you great cuts, as a workout from a gem/gym.

> *Happy is the man that findeth wisdom, and the man that getteth understanding. For the merchandise of it is better than the merchandise of silver, and the gain thereof than fine gold. She is more precious than rubies: and all the things thou canst desire are not to be compared unto her* **(Proverbs 3:13-15)**. *The LORD by wisdom hath founded the earth; by understanding hath he established the heavens. By his knowledge the depths are broken up, and the clouds drop down the dew. My son, let not them departt from thine eyes: keep sound wisdom and discretion: So shall they be life unto thy soul, and grace to thy neck* **(Proverbs 3:19-22)**.

A mirror's image can not change an agreement in prayer. Neither can a mirror's image change a roman numeral 5 (V) to tell/tale/tail a different story.

> *To all that be in Rome, beloved of God, called to be saints: Grace to you and peace from God our Father, and the Lord Jesus Christ* **(Romans 1:7)**.

Grace, that God gives us, will still be grace from a mirror's perspective. But, from a mirror's and water's reflection, when the roman numeral 5 (V) is connected to itself, it Pacifically (specifically) seas/sees as a roman numeral 10 (X) from both sides of the mirror:

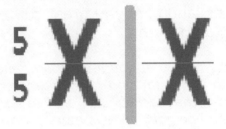

That 5 + 5 is 10, isn't grace also true?

> And the Word was made flesh, and dwelt among us,
> (and we beheld his glory, the glory as of the only
> begotten of the Father,) full of grace and truth. And of
> his fulness have all we received, and grace for grace
> **(John 1:14 and 16)**.

But, when we are stuck on ourselves, all things do not add up correctly:

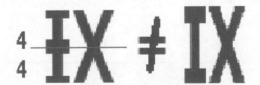

4 + 4 does not equal to 9.

> Then the LORD said unto me, The prophets prophesy
> lies in my name: I sent them not, neither have I
> commanded them, neither spake unto them: they
> prophesy unto you a false vision and divination, and a
> thing of nought, and the deceit of their heart
> **(Jeremiah 14:14)**.

The number 10 stands for perfection and completion. Without grace (V), our lives cannot be complete, and neither can we show a reflection upon perfection:

Moreover, when the grace of praise goes up, then the blessings of grace comes down.

It has been said, "There are two sides to every story." Isn't it amazing how the Father, Son, and Holy Ghost, as a roman numeral 3 (III) image's stories doesn't change, but we do, when we are roman/roaming around, trying to fix things ourselves? If grace, from a mirror's perspective, does not change, and neither does perfection, then why not trust in God to make your life complete?

> *Trust in the LORD with all thine heart; and lean not unto thine own understanding. In all thy ways acknowledge him, and he shall direct thy path* **(Proverbs 3:5-6)**. *The LORD preserveth the strangers; he relieveth the fatherless and widow: but the way of the wicked he turneth upside down* **(Psalm 146:9)**.

"Talk That's Down To Earth Reaching Past Sky Limits"

If you dig into God's word, He will give you understanding to dig what He is saying. Moreover, for you to dig into the word of God, what treasures would you find? Perhaps, if you dig deep enough, you will find the riches of His wisdom beyond the treasures of gold. But, if you don't dig into the word of God, then how can you go deep with God, if you don't dig deep?

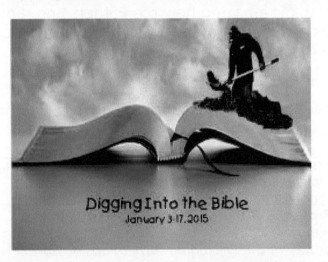

Digging Into the Bible
January 3-17, 2015

And it shall come to pass, if thou shalt hearken diligently unto the voice of the LORD thy God, to obverse and to do all his commandments which I command thee this day, that the LORD thy God will set thee on high above all nations of the earth: And all these blessings shall come on thee, and overtake thee, if thou shalt hearken unto the voice of the LORD thy God (Deuteronomy 28:1-2). Receive my instruction, and not silver; and knowledge rather than choice gold. For wisdom is better than rubies; and all the things that may be desired are not to be compared to it (Proverbs 8:10-11). But it shall come to pass, if thou wilt not hearken unto the voice of the LORD thy God, to observe to do all his commandments and his statutes which I command thee this day; that all these curses shall come upon thee, and overtake thee (Deuteronomy 28:15):

If you want your life to go smooth, then you will have to trust in God by a landslide. But, if you don't put your trust in God by a slide, then would you fall for anything, to slip into someone's mess?

"ON A LANDSLIDE"

Teach me to do thy will; for thou art my God: thy spirit is good; lead me into the land of righteousness. Quicken me, O LORD, for thy name's sake: for thy righteousness' sake bring my soul out of trouble. And of thy mercy cut off mine enemies, and destroy all them that afflict my soul: for I am thy servant (Psalms 143:10-12).

For you to bank on God's trust, you have to know that He is always on the money, because His word is rich and true. Therefore, you should put your account with Him. But, if you don't bank on God's trust, by His word, then poor you. Why trust in man's account, when his statements come back void?

*For the vision is yet for an appointed time, but at the end it shall speak, and not lie: though it tarry, wait for it; because it will surely come, it will not tarry (**Habakkuk 2:3**). So shall my word be that goeth forth out of my mouth: it shall not return unto me void, but it shall accomplish that which I please, and it shall prosper in the thing whereto I sent it (**Isaiah 55:11**).*

If your walk is in the Lord, then you will do some light/life stepping. But, if your walk is not of the Lord, your burdens will be heavy and dark. Therefore, you will not produce life.

*For the LORD God is a sun and shield: the LORD will give grace and glory: no good thing will he withhold from them that walk uprightly **(Psalm 84:11)**. Come unto me, all ye that labour and are heavy laden, and I will give you rest. Take my yoke upon you, and learn of me; for I am meek and lowly in heart: and ye shall find rest unto your souls. For my yoke is easy, and my burden is light **(Matthew 11:28-30)**. And have no fellowship with the unfruitful works of darkness, but rather reprove them **(Ephesians 5:11)**.*

If you want to be on God's schedule to plan every date for your life, then you will have to be in God's plan for every date that He schedules for your life with Him.

*To every thing there is a season, and a time to every purpose under the heaven **(Ecclesiastes 3:1)**: And he said unto them, It is not for you to know the times or the seasons, which the Father hath put in his own power **(Acts 1:7)**. He hath made every thing beautiful in his time: also he hath set the world in their heart, so that no man can find out the work that God maketh from the beginning to the end **(Ecclesiastes 3:11)**.*

God wants us to stand strong in His word, but He also wants us to rest in peace. Now, if we can stand to rest, then we can be a strong peace/piece.

*Therefore, brethren, stand fast, and hold the traditions which ye have been taught, whether by word, or our epistle **(2 Thessalonians 2:15)**. Stand in awe, and sin not: commune with your own heart upon your bed, and be still. I will both lay me down in peace, and sleep: for thou, LORD, only makest me dwell in safety **(Psalms 4:4 and 8)**. The LORD shall fight for you, and ye shall hold your peace **(Exodus 14:14)**.*

If we are God's foundation, then that makes us His business. That we are God's business, then we are incorporated into His plan.

*Nevertheless the foundation of God standeth sure, having this seal, The Lord knoweth them that are his. And, Let every one that nameth the name of Christ depart from iniquity **(2 Timothy 2:19)**. For we are his workmanship, created in Christ Jesus unto good works, which God hath before ordained that we should walk in them **(Ephesians 2:10)**.*

If God has a call on each one of us, then He gave each one of us a number. If we call on God, His number is toll-free/totally free. Therefore, we are mobile with God.

"GOD HAS A CALL FOR YOU. DON'T BET IT ON YOUR LIFE!"

> *He telleth the number of the stars; he calleth them all by their names* **(Psalm 147:4)**. *Let every man abide in the same calling wherein he was called. Art thou called being a servant? care not for it: but if thou mayest be made free, use it rather. For he that is called in the Lord, being a servant, is the Lord's freeman: likewise also he that is called, being free, is Christ's servant. Ye are bought with a price; be not ye the servants of men. Brethren, let every man, wherein he is called, therein abide with God* **(1 Corinthians 7:20-24)**.

If God gives us a will/wheel, then He gives us drive to go high beyond mountains. But, without a drive, what power does your wheel/will have to roll/role?

"A POWER DRIVE FOR FREEDOM AND CAUSE/CALLS FOR YOUR LIFE"

*For it is God which worketh in you both to will and to do of his good pleasure **(Philippians 2:13)**. What shall we then say to these things? If God be for us , who can be against us? He that spared not his own Son, but delivered him up for us all, how shall he not with him also freely give us all things **(Romans 8:31-32)**? Now therefore give me this mountain, whereof the LORD spake in that day; for thou heardest in that day how the Anakims were there, and that the cities were great and fenced: if so be the LORD will be with me, then I shall be able to drive them out, as the LORD said **(Joshua 14:12)**.*

If God makes a statement for each one of our lives, then why not give the Lord a statement, in return, for each morning that we wake up?

*For it is written, AS I LIVE, SAITH THE LORD, EVERY KNEE SHALL BOW TO ME, AND EVERY TONGUE SHALL CONFESS TO GOD **(Romans 14:11)**.*

God wants us to wrap into His word, so that we can rap to others about His word. If we rap to others about God's word, then the Lord will turn our talk into a song.

*Let the word of Christ dwell in you richly in all wisdom; teaching and admonishing one another in psalms and hymns and spirituall songs, singing with grace in your hearts to the Lord **(Colossians 3:16)**.*

God has us in His picture, because we are in his image. That we are in God's image, He can draw us closer to Jesus. If God draws us closer in His picture, then we should be in the frame of God's thinking.

*No man can come to me, except the Father which hath sent me draw him: and I will raise him up at the last day **(John 6:44)**. For he knoweth our frame; he remembereth that we are dust **(Psalm 103:14)**.*

If we are moved by God's will, then we are still in the will of God. But, if we are still by the will of God, then how can we be moved?

THE TEN COMMANDMENTS

1. I AM THE LORD YOUR GOD. YOU SHALL WORSHIP THE LORD YOUR GOD AND HIM ONLY SHALL YOU SERVE.

2. YOU SHALL NOT TAKE THE NAME OF THE LORD YOUR GOD IN VAIN.

3. REMEMBER TO KEEP HOLY THE SABBATH DAY.

4. HONOR YOUR FATHER AND YOUR MOTHER.

5. YOU SHALL NOT KILL.

6. YOU SHALL NOT COMMIT ADULTERY.

7. YOU SHALL NOT STEAL.

8. YOU SHALL NOT BEAR FALSE WITNESS.

9. YOU SHALL NOT COVET YOUR NEIGHBOR'S WIFE.

10. YOU SHALL NOT COVET YOUR NEIGHBOR'S GOODS.

If we are still in the will of God, then we are firm to His writes/rights.

*For the prophecy came not in old time by the will of man: but holy men of God spake as they were moved by the Holy Ghost **(2 Peter 1:21)**. A man shall not be established by wickedness: but the root of the righteous shall not be moved **(Proverbs 12:3)**.*

If you are at the right hand of God, then you won't be left out, because being at God's right hand, you can't go wrong.

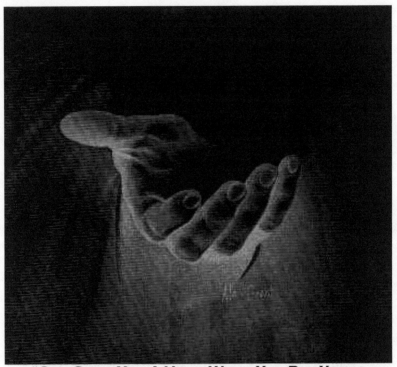

"GOD GIVES YOU A HAND WHEN YOU PUT YOURS TOGETHER IN PRAYER/PRAISE!"

*Therefore being by the right hand of God exalted, and having received of the Father the promise of the Holy Ghost, he hath shed forth this, which ye now see and hear **(Acts 2:33)**. Let your conversation be without covetousness; and be content with such things as ye have: for he hath said, I WILL NEVER LEAVE THEE, NOR FORSAKE THEE **(Hebrews 13:5)**.*

Doctors on Earth will provide you with medication of many negative side effects. But, the medication/meditation of God's word has positive side effects for your life, prescribed by Doctor Jesus.

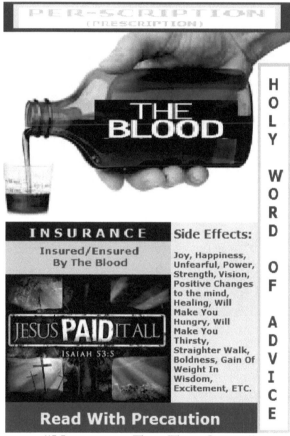

"MEDICINE FOR THE SOUL"

*And said, If thou wilt diligently hearken to the voice of the LORD thy God, and wilt do that which is right in his sight, and wilt give ear to his commandments, and keep all his statutes, I will put none of these diseases upon thee, which I have brought upon the Egyptians: for I am the LORD that healeth thee **(Exodus 15:26)**.*

When Jesus knocks on your door, do you open up opportunity, or do you opt out of His plan? If you don't answer to the knock of the Lord, then whose hand will you trust if it is balled up to knock you down?

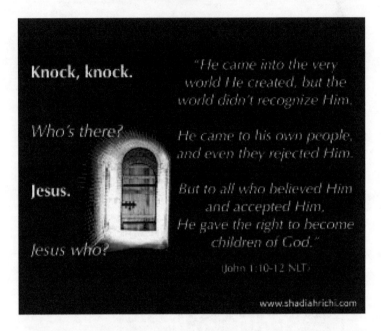

Behold, I stand at the door, and knock: if any man hear my voice, and open the door, I will come in to him, and will sup with him, and he with me **(Revelation 3:20)**. *Of the Rock that begat thee thou art unmindful, and hast forgotten God that formed thee. And when the LORD saw it, he abhorred them, because of the provoking of his sons, and of his daughters. And he said, I will hide my face from them, I will see what their end shall be: for they are a very froward generation, children in whom is no faith* **(Deuteronomy 32:18-20)**. *Put not your trust in princes, nor in the son of man, in whom there is no help* **(Psalm 146:3)**.

The Son of God died on the cross to save our lives, by His might. When we, as Christians, go to the house of the Lord to celebrate the resurrection of Jesus, isn't He the light of the party? But, if Jesus never came to Cross, in our path, then perhaps, we would have all been dyna-mite, without being a J. Walker (jay walker), and having no "Good Times".

(JIMMIE WALKER IS J J FROM THE SITCOM "GOOD TIMES". HE ALWAYS SAYS, "DYNO-MITE"!)

*It was meet that we should make merry, and be glad: for this thy brother was dead, and is alive again; and was lost, and is found **(Luke 15:32)**. Nay, in all these things we are more than conquerors through him that loved us. For I am persuaded, that neither death, nor life, nor angels, nor principalities, nor powers, nor things present, nor things to come, Nor height, nor depth, nor any other creature, shall be able to separate us from the love of God, which Is in Christ Jesus our Lord **(Romans 8:37-39)**. There is therefore now no condemnation to them which are in Christ Jesus, who walk not after the flesh, but after the Spirit **(Romans 8:1)**.*

If "THE LORD'S RICHEST" is all capital, then "HE" has no lower case, because HE is the Highest Judge over all Judges that will ever come Across/A Cross truly.

"TO BE LIKE JESUS, WE HAVE TO COME ACROSS/A CROSS IN HIS PATH. THEREFORE, WE ALL HAVE TO LINE UP WITH HIM."

*But he that is spiritual judgeth all things, yet he himself is judged of no man (**1 Corinthians 2:15**). The LORD standeth up to plead, and standeth to judge the people (**Isaiah 3:13**). For we know him that hath said, VENGEANCE BELONGETH UNTO ME, I WILL RECOMPENSE, saith the Lord. And again, THE LORD SHALL JUDGE HIS PEOPLE (**Hebrews 10:30**).*

If God's word gives us coverage, then why trust in man's word that will put us into the open, and that is not written? If man has no signature to his word, then why not trust in God, who is the author and finisher of our lives, through signs and wonders?

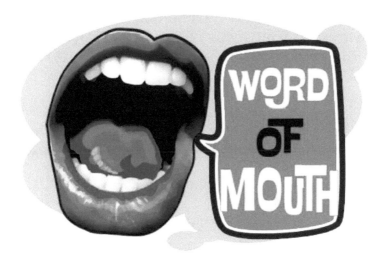

If the tongue can cut like a sword, then why believe in the words of man, when Jesus already sacrificed His blood for our lives?

*O GOD the Lord, the strength of my salvation, thou hast covered my head in the day of battle **(Psalm 140:7)**. It is better to trust in the LORD than to put confidence in man **(Psalm 118:8)**. Looking unto Jesus the author and finisher of our faith; who for the joy that was set before him endured the cross, despising the shame, and is set down at the right hand of the throne of God **(Hebrews 12:2)**.*

Each one of us can be a Starr/star in Chirst Jesus. We can light up as a Starr/star, because Jesus puts a light in each one of us. Therefore, Jesus is THE SUPERSTAR/SUPER STARR, because HE is THE SON/SUN that shed HIS blood to give us light. Isn't it amazing how we get mad with a red light, and not know that it's Jesus sitting us still, at a "Cross Street", to talk with us? That Jesus is THE SUPERSTAR/SUPER STARR, then why not SUP with HIM, to operate in the SUPERNATURAL?

> *Behold, I stand at the door and knock: if any man hear my voice, and open the door, I will come in to him, and will sup with him, and he with me **(Revelation 3:20)**.*

If Jesus is my rock, then I can roll/role with Him. If I stick with the Lord, as I am in His image, then we can rock-n-roll/role together.

> *The LORD is my rock, and my fortress, and my deliverer; my God, my strength, in whom I will trust; my buckler, and the horn of my salvation, and my high tower. I will call upon the LORD, who is worthy to be praised so shall I be saved from mine enemies **(Psalms 18:2-3)**.*

"Power Of An Animal's Prey Versus Our Pray"

It's amazing how an animal will go hunting boldly, everyday to search for their prey. They make it their priority. Why is it so hard for us to find the time to prioritize our hunt boldly, to search through God's word, to find what we should pray? If we are hungry for the word of God, will not He feed us and lead us to what we should pray for, through the bread of His word? Since we must not live by bread alone, we will also be fed by the meat of His word? Doesn't God make us His priority above all animals?

*The young lions roar after their prey, and seek their meat from God **(Psalm 104:21)**. And God said, Let us make man in our image, after our likeness: and let them have dominion over the fish of the sea, and over the fowl of the air, and over the cattle, and over all the earth, and over every creeping thing that creepeth upon the earth **(Genesis 1:26)**. And I will give you shepherds according to My heart, who will feed you with knowledge and understanding **(Jeremiah 3:15 NKJV)**. And Jesus said unto them, I am the bread of life: he that cometh to me shall never hunger; and he that believeth on me shall never thirst **(John 6:35)**. But he answered and said, It is written, MAN SHALL NOT LIVE BY BREAD ALONE, BUT BY EVERY WORD THAT PROCEEDETH OUT OF THE MOUTH OF GOD **(Matthew 4:4)**.*

How is it that animals which are larger than we are, will make us move,

"ARE WE MOVED BY ANIMALS?"

when God has given us the power to move mountains that are humongous over all animals?

And Jesus said unto them, Because of your unbelief: for verily I say unto you, If ye have faith as a grain of mustard seed, ye shall say unto this mountain, Remove hence to yonder place; and it shall remove; and nothing shall be impossible unto you **(Matthew 17:20)**.

Furthermore, how come animals that are smaller than we are, will come to attack us, and make us move?

BY THE LOOKS OF IT, IS HE GIVING PRAISE BY FEAR OF A SMALL CREATURE THAT SNAKED UP/SNEAKED UP ON HIM? BUT, WE ARE SUPPOSED TO ONLY FEAR AND PRAISE GOD.

The fear of the LORD is the beginning of knowledge: but fools despise wisdom and instruction ***(Proverbs 1:7)****.
And fear not them which kill the body, but are not able to kill the soul: but rather fear him which is able to destroy both soul and body in hell* ***(Matthew 10:28)****.
And the LORD commanded us to do all these statutes, to fear the LORD our God, for our good always, that he might preserve us alive, as it is at this day* ***(Deuteronomy 6:24)****.*

Are we in their territory, or did God give us this land to walk freely?

And God made the beast of the earth after his kind, and cattle after their kind, and every thing that creepeth upon the earth after his kind: and God saw that it was good. And God said, Let us make man in our image, after our likeness: and let them have dominion over the fish of the sea, and over the fowl of the air, and over the cattle, and over all the earth, and

*over every creeping thing that creepeth upon the earth.
So God created man in his own image, in the image of
God created he him; male and female created he them.
And God blessed them, and God said unto them, Be
fruitful, and multiply, and replenish the earth, and
subdue it: and have dominion over the fish of the sea,
and over the fowl of the air, and over every living thing
that moveth upon the earth **(Genesis 1:25-28)**.
Arise, walk through the land in the length of it and in
the breadth of it; for I will give it unto thee
(Genesis 13:17).*

Therefore, we should stand strong over all living
animals, and shall not be moved. If you cannot stand
to be still, then perhaps, you are living through a
wildlife/wild life.

*But ask now the beasts, and they shall teach thee; and
the fowls of the air, and they shall tell thee: Or speak
to the earth, and it shall teach thee; and the fishes of
the sea shall declare unto thee: Who knoweth not in
all these that the hand of the LORD hath wrought this?
In whose hand is the soul of every living thing, and the
breath of all mankind **(Job 12:7-10)**.*

207

Do you have the faith to walk across a sea/see of waters? Can you make the waters cease, to be still? If you can walk on the waters farther than Peter, then you can beat a pool shark.

But, if you can walk as far as Jesus walked on the waters, and not loose your faith, then you can take on a sea shark.

And straightway Jesus constrained his disciples to get into a ship, and to go before him unto the other side, while he sent the multitude away. And when he had

sent the multitudes away, he went up into a mountain apart to pray: and when the evening was come, he was there alone. But the ship was now in the midst of the sea, tossed with weaves: for the wind was contrary. And in the fourth watch of the night Jesus went unto them, walking on the sea. And when the disciples saw him walking on the sea, they were troubled, saying, It is a spirit; and they cried out for fear. But straightway Jesus spake unto them, saying, Be of good cheer; it is I; be not afraid. And Peter answered him and said, Lord, if it be thou, bid me come unto thee on the water. And he said, Come. And when Peter was come down out of the ship, he walked on the water, to go to Jesus. But when he saw the wind boisterous, he was afraid; and beginning to sink, he cried, saying, Lord, save me. And immediately Jesus stretched forth his hand, and caught him, and said unto him, O thou of little saith, wherefore didst thou doubt (Matthew 14:22-31)?

Isn't it amazing how animals don't fast, so they won't miss their prey time?

Wilt thou hunt the prey for the lion? or fill the appetite of the young lions, When they couch in their dens, and abide in the covert to lie in wait? Who provideth for the raven his food? when his young ones cry unto God, they wander for lack of meat (Job 38:39-41).

But, when we fast to glorify God, it's funny how we want time to go by quickly from a fast time. If we fast for the Lord, then what's the rush? Now, when we finish fasting, to sacrifice for the Lord, and it is now time to eat, how many of us will remember to pray beforehand? Perhaps, your hands will gravitate towards your food before you remember to pray.

*I thank my God, making mention of thee always in my prayers **(Philemon 1:4)**. Whether therefore ye eat, or drink, or whatsoever ye do, do all to the glory of God **(1 Corinthians 10:31)**. And when he had thus spoken, he took bread, and gave thanks to God in presence of them all: and when he had broken it, he began to eat **(Acts 27:35)**.*

But, that we have dominion over all animals, it's also amazing that many animals under us will not forget to pray? Grace be on to them!

"CAT PRAYING BEFORE A CATNAP"

And the first beast was like a lion, and the second beast like a calf, and the third beast had a face as a man, and the fourth beast was like a flying eagle. And the four beasts had each of them six wings about him; and they were full of eyes within: and they rest not day and night, saying, Holy, holy, holy, Lord God Almighty, which was, and is, and is to come. And when those beasts give glory and honour and thanks to him that sat on the throne, who liveth for ever and ever, The four and twenty elders fall down before him that sat on the throne, and worship him that liveth for ever and ever, and cast their crowns before the throne, saying, Thou art worthy, O Lord, to receive glory and honour and power: for thou hast created all things, and for thy pleasure they are and were created **(Revelation 4:7-11)**.

I wonder why this is called a doggy-dog world? Maybe, when their praises go up, blessings are coming down for them. If you let the trees of the field out praise you, when you're sitting down watching TV or in bed sleeping, do you also let the dogs out praise you, to takeover your blessings?

"DOG GETTING ITS PRAISE ON"

For dogs and cats to be loyal to their master's, aren't they blessed when God is raining cats and dogs?

Perhaps, their gifts are being multiplied for being true to their master's.

"RAINING CATS & DOGS"

But, when God reigns over us, do we remain loyal to Him? When dogs show their joy with a dance, do they dance as David danced? But, when we, as humans, show our joy for the Lord, why don't we do our dance like David? Isn't it amazing how we can learn from animals? They can teach us in many ways. Many of us have learned how to write in "Chicken scratch". We have that handwriting down to a science, especially those who are doctors.

DR. DOG IS TIED UP IN CLASS SESSION AT THE MOMENT.

Some animals have been blessed to become Movie Stars. Perhaps, they had high beliefs and high expectations, but yet, they remained loyal. But we, on the other hand, our faith seems to stop, and doubt enters in, right before our blessing comes. It's as if we're running from our blessings in fear, like we're running from the animals that are supposed to fear us. Therefore, if animals that are bigger or smaller than we are, can make us fear, by removing our faith, then what power do we have left to move our mountains, in which the Lord gave us dominion over? Moreover, if there is power in wisdom, then our schedule should be booked with a lot to learn, day by day.

"HAVING A BOOKED SCHEDULE"

And the fear of you and the dread of you shall be upon every beast of the earth, and upon every fowl of the air, upon all that moveth upon the earth, and upon all the fishes of the sea; into your hand are they delivered. Every moving thing that liveth shall be meat for you; even as the green herb have I given you all things **(Genesis 9:2-3)**.

"Will You Let A Tree Out Praise You"

It's something how trees will give their highest praise when they are left out in the cold. They turn to no one.

*Then shall the trees of the wood sing out at the presence of the LORD, because he cometh to judge the earth **(1 Chronicles 16:33)**.*

On the contrary, if trees will turn to know one, they can be partners in prime, and have a great merry life together, as a "Tree Family" (That's taking a spinoff from "Family Tree"), branch together as a "Double Tree", having a Holy-tale Praise (spinoff from Double

214

Tree Hotel), as they have a vocation in agreement. It looks like trees have made names for themselves.

THE TREES ARE BANKING ON A BRANCH TO LEAN ON. IF WE CAN BANK ON A BRANCH, LIKE TREES, WE WOULD ALL BE RICH, WITH FULL OF GREEN, GROWING AT OUR BRANCH.

*For he shall be as a tree planted by the waters, and that spreadeth out her roots by the river, and shall not see when heat cometh, but her leaf shall be green; and shall not be careful in the year of drought, neither shall cease from yielding fruit **(Jeremiah 17:8)**. For there is hope of a tree, if it be cut down, that it will sprout again, and that the tender branch thereof will not cease **(Job 14:7)**.*

A group of trees will log together to branch out in praise, even with no cloves/clothes on. Moreover, when their branches of wealth, has no green, it's

215

amazing, that in those seasons, trees stay focused, and not look to each other. They continue to stand strong through their coldest seasons, and branch out to the Lord, with their hardest/harvest praise, for a windy/winning battle. Isn't it also amazing how trees can have leaves of absence, and not forget to branch out to God through praise?

"TREES BRANCHING OUT IN PRAISE THROUGH A COLD SEASON"

*Neither is there any creature that is not manifest in his sight: but all things are naked and opened unto the eyes of him with whom we have to do. Seeing then that we have a great high priest, that is passed into the heavens, Jesus the Son of God, let us hold fast our profession. For we have not an high priest which cannot be touched with the feeling of our infirmities; but was in all points tempted like as we are, yet without sin **(Hebrews 4:13-15)**. Then shall the trees of the wood sing out at the presence of the LORD, because he cometh to judge the earth **(1 Chronicles 16:33)**.*

Trees will take a big hit, and continue to glorify God, right where they fall. Is that the reason why trees are filled with many fruits?

And God said, Behold, I have given you every herb bearing seed, which is upon the face of all the earth, and every tree, in the which is the fruit of a tree yielding seed; to you it shall be for meat **(Genesis 1:29)**.

Trees share their fruits with us, and not complain. Perhaps, that's why trees continue to grow more fruit, by seeds that were planted through them?

Ye shall know them by their fruits. Do men gather grapes of thorns, or figs of thistles? Even so every good tree bringeth forth good fruit; but a corrupt tree bringeth forth evil fruit. A good tree cannot bring forth evil fruit, neither can a corrupt tree bring forth good fruit. Every tree that bringeth not forth good fruit is hewn down, and cast into the fire. Wherefore by their fruits ye shall know them **(Matthew 7:16-20)**.

But, on the other hand, when we are treated cold, in many circumstances, we tend to let our praise down, and hold to ourselves.

Instead of getting down with praise for the Lord, our guards come up. On that note, do we also let God down, instead of trusting in Him? We turn to man for help instead of turning to our Lord. Do we hate to praise the Lord in the form that we came into this world, when we are by ourselves, or do we have a tendency to cover up our truths with what we lie on?

> *Then Job arose, and rent his mantle, and shaved his head, and fell down upon the ground, and worshipped, And said, Naked came I out of my mother's womb, and naked shall I return thither: the LORD gave, and the LORD hath taken away; blessed be the name of the LORD* ***(Job 1:20-21)***.

Why is it that we have a tendency to cover up what God has made us to be, for wrong reasons? But, on the contrary, many of us will reveal our truths for the wrong reasons, without a praise. But, are people stuck on themselves in a mirror, and giving praise for who they are, more so than the grace of God.

Do we forget about our praise for the Lord?

We then that are strong ought to bear the infirmities of the weak, and not to please ourselves. Let every one of us please his neighbour for his good to edification **(Romans 15:1-2)**. *I have shewed you all things, how that so labouring ye ought to support the weak, and to remember the words of the Lord Jesus, how he said, It is more blessed to give than to receive* **(Acts 20:35)**. *There is that scattereth, and yet increaseth; and there is that withholdeth more than is meet, but it tendeth to poverty* **(Proverbs 11:24)**.

*That thine alms may be in secret: and thy Father which seeth in secret himself shall reward thee openly. And when thou prayest, thou shalt not be as the hypocrites are: for they love to pray standing in the synagogues and in the corners of the streets, that they may be seen of men. Verily I say unto you, They have their reward. But thou, when thou prayest, enter into thy closet, and when thou hast shut thy door, pray to thy Father which is in secret; and thy Father which seeth in secret shall reward thee openly **(Matthew 6:4-6)**. That the trial of your faith, being much more precious than of gold that perisheth, though it be tried with fire, might be found unto praise and honour and glory at the appearing of Jesus Christ **(1 Peter 1:7)**:*

We will take a leave of absence from church, and we tend to forget to branch out, to connect to the Lord. We will take a big hit in salary, and continue to look down with no continued praise. But, if we have a big hit in a fist fight, we want to lay hands on the other person, with no intentions of healing.

*Rejoicing in hope; patient in tribulation; continuing instant in prayer **(Romans 12:12)**; And let us not be weary in well doing: for in due season we shall reap, if we faint not **(Galatians 6:9)**. Now I beseech you, brethren, mark them which cause divisions and offences contrary to the doctrine which ye have learned; and avoid them **(Romans 16:17)**.*

It's something how we, as brothers and sisters in Christ, hate to share. Is that the reason why many fruits are not shown through us? Maybe, it's that we complain about what we do/what is due, or what we do not have. Is that our excuse not to praise God? Perhaps, that's why we feel no need to sow a seed.

Isn't it something how trees reach higher than us, but God gives us dominion over all trees?

> *Do all things without murmurings and disputings* **(Philippians 2:14)**: *Let no corrupt communication proceed out of your mouth, but that which is good to the use of edifying, that it may minister grace unto the hearers* **(Ephesians 4:29)**.

Isn't it funny how a tree will go through a fall and winter season, and continue by standing strong?

"A TREE STANDING STRONG WHILE SEASONED WITH SNOW"

It's also amazing how trees are grounded in their room place, for their entire lives, and they continue to give God praise, as they stand strong. That's why trees are winners during a crisis? But, God has made us to be strong through Christ, so that we can also be winners. But, when we are grounded in our rooms, just for a short moment, we tend to loose our joy, and have no praise for our God. Therefore, we fall short of praise, and we loose what we stand for. A tree will continue in praise, right where they fall, unless all of their branches are cutoff. Then, they would have no one to log onto for worship. Perhaps, the burglar had stolen the tree's armor/army of branches. Therefore, the burden would be too heavy for it to praise. But, our arms, that are as thick as a log, of a smaller tree, God still provides us access to worship. God has bestowed into us, our whole arms/armor. We can even connect with our brothers and sisters In Christ, as an army of soldiers.

"BRANCHING TO NEIGHBORS IN PRAYER BY ARMED FORCES"

Furthermore, if you want to get technical with our Father in Heaven, through technology, we can log onto God's word from an electric device (computer, iPod, or cell phone). Therefore, how can we run out of energy for the Lord, when we have the power source of Wi-Fi, that's 24/7, having no leaf/leave of absences, to help us branch out beyond the measure of trees?

> *Every branch in me that beareth not fruit he taketh away: and every branch that beareth fruit, he purgeth it, that it may bring forth more fruit. Abide in me, and I in you. As the branch cannot bear fruit of itself, except it abide in the vine; no more can ye abide in me. I am the vine, ye are the branches: He that abideth in me, and I in him, the same bringeth forth much fruit: for without me ye can do nothing. If a man abide not in me, he is cast forth as a branch, and is withered; and men gather them, and cast them into the fire, and they are burned (John 15:2 and 4-6). Then I will give you rain in due season, and the land shall yield her increase, and the trees of the field shall yield their fruit (Leviticus 26:4).*

"Having Leftovers"

One Afternoon I went to a client's house. The husband was very grouchy. His wife asked me, "Will you like to have lunch?" I answered, "Yes ma'am!" The husband responded, "We're having leftovers." I said, "Great! Food taste better when it's marinated over night." We also have food from God's word that has been marinated for centuries. It is the best food that we can live on. The blood raises the taste to perpetual elevations that accepts no margarine/margins.

WHEN JESUS' BLOOD RAISES THE TASTE, IT ALSO RAISES THE PRICE THAT WAS PAID FOR OUR SINS.

*For my flesh is meat indeed, and my blood is drink indeed. He that eateth my flesh, and drinketh my blood, dwelleth in me, and I in him. As the living Father hath sent me, and I live by the Father: so he that eateth me, even he shall live by me. This is that bread which came down from heaven: not as your fathers did eat man'-na, and are dead: he that eateth of this bread shall live for ever (**John 6:55-58**).*

This food has a priceless value, because it marinades over time, but the Lord gives it to us for free. The more we partake or take part in His word, it seems to get better and better, the more we get into it. That's because He wants to bring the taste to life, with us in the midst of His seasons.

It's amazing how we can marinade in Psalms of His word, but leaving nothing behind.

The Lord wants us to get into the heart of His word, and anoint us with oil. Why not get braised up (fired up)/praised up in God's word, so that He can doctor us up in His seasons, to live eternal life, where we can continue to be raised from glory to glory?

> *I will meditate also of all thy work; and talk of thy doings (Psalm 77:12). Preach the word; be instant in season, out of season; reprove, rebuke, exhort with all longsuffering and doctrine (2 Timothy 4:2).*

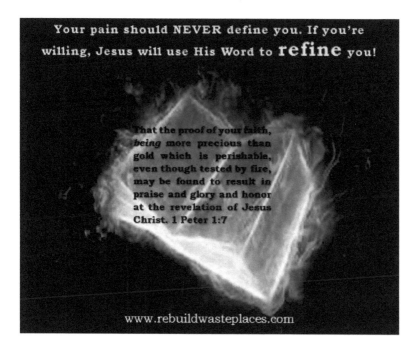

Your pain should NEVER define you. If you're willing, Jesus will use His Word to **refine** you!

That the proof of your faith, *being* more precious than gold which is perishable, even though tested by fire, may be found to result in praise and glory and honor at the revelation of Jesus Christ. 1 Peter 1:7

www.rebuildwasteplaces.com

*That the trial of your faith, being much more precious than of gold that perisheth, though it be tried with fire, might be found unto praise and honour and glory at the appearing of Jesus Christ (**1 Peter 1:7**):*

We have to stand firm in the source of God's word. The source of God's word is the sauce of His word. In order to stand firm into the word of God, you will have to be heated for his order. Most of the sauces for food are hot or spicy. The word of the Lord is also food. Rather stay heated into the word of God, than to stay heated into this world. To be heated into the source of God's word is to also stand firm into the sauce of His word. That the Word of God is the "A1 Source", when you dip into it, you're also dipping into His "A1 Sauce". You are to stand firm as the meat of God's word. When you dip into God's sauce, perhaps, you look good for the world to chew you out. That's why you have to be a tough meat, as a Christian. Therefore, you can not be tender.

> *Finally, my brethren, be strong in the Lord, and in the power of his might. Put on the whole armour of God, that ye may be able to stand against the wiles of the devil* **(Ephesians 6:10-11)**.

"Reverse Word-ology"

We will have a moment when we go THROUGH to a BREAK, but after we've had our BREAKTHROUGH.

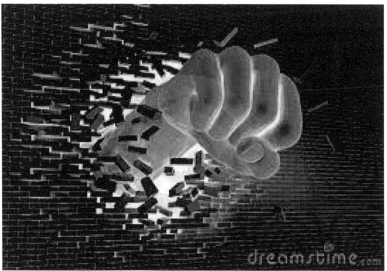

"A BREAKTHROUGH TO A BREAK"

*For we which have believed do enter into rest, as he said, AS I HAVE SWORN IN MY WRATH, IF THEY SHALL ENTER INTO MY REST: although the works were finished from the foundation of the world **(Hebrews 4:3)**. There remaineth therefore a rest to the people of God. For he that is entered into his rest, he also hath ceased from his own works, as God did from his **(Hebrews 4:9-10)**.*

When you go on a TRIP, do you MIND having a lot of LUGGAGE, or do you have a lot of LUGGAGE in your MIND when you TRIP?

"DO YOU WALK AROUND TRIPPING WITH A LOT OF LUGGAGE?"

*Remember ye not the former things, neither consider the things of old **(Isaiah 43:18)**. Brethren, I count not myself to have apprehended: but this one thing I do, forgetting those things which are behind, and reaching forth unto those things which are before, I press toward the mark for the prize of the high calling of God in Christ Jesus **(Philippians 3:13-14)**.*

If you HOLD ON, to the Lord by faith, faith by the Lord will not put you ON HOLD.

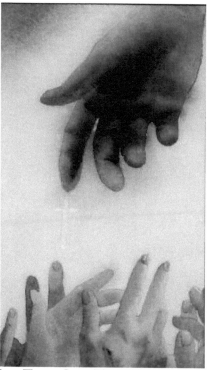

"IF YOU TELL GOD TO HOLD ON, THEN HE WILL PUT YOU ON HOLD"

*And the L*ORD *shall guide thee continually, and satisfy thy soul in drought, and make fat thy bones: and thou shalt be like a watered garden, and like a spring of water, whose waters fail not* **(Isaiah 58:11)**. *There hath no temptation taken you but such as is common to man: but God is faithful, who will not suffer you to be tempted above that ye are able; but will with the temptation also make a way to escape, that ye may be able to bear it* **(1 Corinthians 10:13)**.

If you don't have SUCCESSFUL KEYS to open the doors, then how can you have the KEYS to open doors to FULL SUCCESS/FULFILL SUCCESS?

"THE KEY TO SUCCESS"

*Ask, and it shall be given you; seek, and ye shall find; knock, and it shall be opened unto you: For every one that asketh receiveth; and he that seeketh findeth; and to him that knocketh it shall be opened (**Matthew 7:7-8**). I am the door: by me if any man enter in, he shall be saved, and shall go in and out, and find pasture (**John 10:9**). And I will give unto thee the keys of the kingdom of heaven: and whatsoever thou shalt bind on earth shall be bound in heaven: and whatsoever thou shalt loose on earth shall be loosed in heaven (**Matthew 16:19**).*

We can't STAND IN, by being OUT from the crowd, so we have to STAND OUT IN a crowd before we can be OUTSTANDING to a crowd.

"BECOME OUTSTANDING TO STANDOUT!"

And Jesus departed from thence, and came nigh unto the sea of Galilee; and went up into a mountain, and sat down there. And great multitudes came unto him, having with them those that were lame, blind, dumb, maimed, and many others, and cast them down at Jesus' feet; and he healed them: Insomuch that the multitude wondered, when they saw the dumb to speak, the maimed to be whole, the lame to walk, and the blind to see: and they glorified the God of Israel **(Matthew 15:29-31)**.

When you are LET OUT to experience life, to whom do you put your trust, to be the power source for your OUTLET?

*The preparations of the heart in man, and the answer of the tongue, is from the LORD. All the ways of a man are clean in his own eyes; but the LORD weigheth the spirits. Commit thy works unto the LORD, and thy thoughts shall be established. The LORD hath made all things for himself: yea, even the wicked for the day of evil. Every one that is proud in heart is an abomination to the LORD: though hand join in hand, he shall not be unpunished **(Proverbs 16:1-5)**.*

Just because you CAREFULLY LOOK OUT through life, doesn't mean that you will FULLY CARE for the OUTLOOK of life.

However the best news is that even if you are more prone to negativity, there are things you can do to change your mind set and give you a wonderful outlook on life.

*Whereas ye know not what shall be on the morrow. For what is your life? It is even a vapour, that appeareth for a little time, and then vanisheth away. For that ye ought to say, If the Lord will, we shall live, and do this, or that (**James 4:14-15**). O LORD, I know that the way of man is not in himself: it is not in man that walketh to direct his steps (**Jeremiah 10:23**).*

Just because you're SET UP to take a PICTURE on a cloudy day, doesn't mean that you have to PICTURE yourself, on a cloudy day, being UPSET.

Wherefore seeing we also are compassed about with so great a cloud of witnesses, let us lay aside every weight, and the sin which doth so easily beset us, and let us run with patience the race that is set before us, Looking unto Jesus the author and finisher of our faith; who for the joy that was set before him endured the cross, despising the shame, and is set down at the right hand of the throne of God **(Hebrews 12:1-2)**.

When we do things by GOD'S TIMING, then we don't
do things by TIMING GOD.

*For the vision is yet for an appointed time, but at the
end it shall speak, and not lie: though it tarry, wait for
it; because it will surely come, it will not tarry*
(Habakkuk 2:3).

If you LIVE, flowing in the word of God, then the word
of God that flows out of you is LIVE (līv), and not
EVIL.

*He that believeth on me, as the scripture hath said, out
of his belly shall flow rivers of living water* **(John
7:38)**.

"On One Accord With The Lord"

If we get on one accord with the Lord, then you will be shocked, with the electricity of God's miracles for our enlightenment. He reigns/rains over us when we are going through the storms of life.

"GETTING SHOCKED BY GOD'S ENLIGHTMENT"

*The LORD of hosts is with us; the God of Jacob is our refuge. Selah **(Psalm 46:11)**. The LORD reigneth; let the earth rejoice; let the multitude of isles be glad thereof. Clouds and darkness are round about him: righteousness and judgment are the habitation of his throne **(Psalms 97:1-2)**.*

To be on God's one accord, when we stand through Satan's wired up scams, our electricity will be strong enough to endure Satan's shocking moments. The power strength of his mini/many cords (schemes) will not out last God's power cord for our lives. As long as we stay plugged in to His Word, our strength will apparently be magnified, because God is the best parent that we can have. Isn't it amazing how something that's apparently seen is truly seen? Well, God, our Father, is all truth.

"Go Accordance/According To God's Word. Moreover, If You Go AC Cording With God's Word, You Will Stay Cool As A Fan Of God."

Put on the whole armour of God, that ye may be able to stand against the wiles of the devil. For we wrestle not against flesh and blood, but against principalities, against powers, against the rulers of the darkness of this world, against spiritual wickedness in high places.

*Wherefore take unto you the whole armour of God, that ye may be able to withstand in the evil day, and having done all, to stand. Stand therefore, having your loins girt about with truth, and having on the breastplate of righteousness; And your feet shod with the preparation of the gospel of peace; Above all, taking the shield of faith, wherewith ye shall be able to quench all the fiery darts of the wicked. And take the helmet of salvation, and the sword of the Spirit, which is the word of God **(Ephesians 6:11-17)**:*

Don't buy into Satan's electric currents, because God has the best/blessed plan for our current time. God's electricity has everlasting life, whereas Satan's electricity will soon go dead.

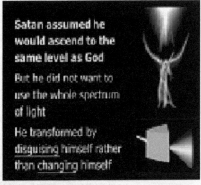

VS

"GOD'S CURRENT TIME"   **"SATAN'S ELECTRIC CURRENT"**

*Ye are of God, little children, and have overcome them: because greater is he that is in you, than he that is in the world **(1 John 4:4)**. Behold, I give unto you power to tread on serpents and scorpions, and over all the power of the enemy: and nothing shall by any means hurt you **(Luke 10:19)**.*

Through the power source of God, we can all be charged with more energy for life. But, the charge of

Satan's schemes would have us wired-up/fired-up through a bad connection, as a battery against us, doing life in prison, with an underground nation.

"CHARGED WITH A BATTERY AGAINST HIM"

The evil promotions of Satan's schemes are all his volt/fault. That Satan doesn't have any light in his volt, there is no wonder why we may not see our own mistakes. If we don't have watt/what it takes in these evil times, then the Lord will enlighten us through prayer. Moreover, do you have watt/what it takes to see the light at the other end of the tunnel, to build your vision? If you don't have watt/what it takes, to structure your vision, your drive may be in darkness. If you can't see your journey ahead, then you will have to revolt from a default, to see from a better light. Perhaps, you are working through a rush hour, and creating your drive with a time window for your vision, because you want things to happen quickly. Has that caused you to miss your turn for your blessing and calling? Maybe, you are working through blindness, by the shield of your window, to keep away the sun/Son and the light. If we confess our dark volts/faults to The Lord, He will bring us a-bulb/above the rest, for light, over Satan's darkness. The Lord just wants us to rest in Him. If you will get rest in God, then God extends guidance to you for the rest of your life by His will.

"PRAYING WATT/WHAT IT TAKES TO SEE THE LIGHT A-BULB (ABOVE)"

*Whereunto I also labour, striving according to his working, which worketh in me mightily **(Colossians 1:29)**. Be careful for nothing; but in every thing by prayer and supplication with thanksgiving let your requests be made known unto God **(Philippians 4:6)**.*

And your life would be brighter than noonday. Though you were dark, you would be like the morning. And you would be secure, because there is hope; Yes, you would dig around you, and take your rest in safety **(Job 11:17-18 NKJV)**. *If ye abide in me, and my words abide in you, ye shall ask what ye will, and it shall be done unto you* **(John 15:7)**.

If you plug into Satan's outlet, his fire will not let out. Now, if you plug into God's outlet, you will have electrifying joy for eternity. The lighting of God's voltage is forevermore,

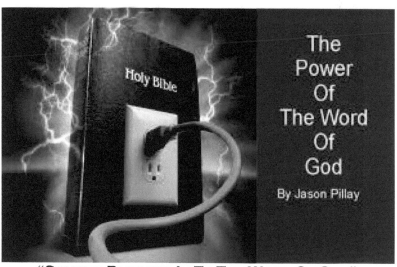

"STAYING PLUGGED IN TO THE WORD OF GOD"

but Satan's voltage is not even pure darkness, because nothing about Satan is pure. Satan operates in total darkness. It's amazing how we enjoy the electricity of our mates, and not recommend God who blessed us, and measured us with the pleasure. With the Lord, we have a true mate in Heaven, so why not gravitate to the power of the Lord, like a magnet?

"IF YOU WILL BE STILL/STEEL, IN THE WORD OF GOD, YOU'LL SEE HOW GOD WILL CONNECT TO YOU LIKE A MAGNET"

Now unto him that is able to do exceeding abundantly above all that we ask or think, according to the power that worketh in us, Unto him be glory in the church by Christ Jesus throughout all ages, world without end. Amen (Ephesians 3:20-21).

38 Magnets

ABOUT THE AUTHOR

With the publication of Brandon T. Mitchell's third novel, He has many unique flowing thoughts that the Lord, God, births into his mind, day by day. As they become overwhelming, he wants to share his knowledge with others. Brandon T. Mitchell, at many times, was misunderstood, but his educational background proves him to be more advanced than what many individuals labeled him to be. He has a Bachelor's Degree from Tennessee State University in Family and Consumer Sciences with a Concentration in Interior Design, and a MBA in Accounting with a 4.0 GPA from Jones International University. Many down falls in the past has only made Brandon T. Mitchell a stronger person in life. He is a fighter for what he believes, and never gives up on his dreams.